BECOMING WORSHIP

DISCOVERING OUR TRUE IDENTITY

by
ALANDERSON CARVALHO

FOREWORD

I count it a privilege to know Alanderson Carvalho. He practices what he teaches by not only ministering from a platform, but living it privately, too.

I first met Alan in 2010. We were then both 'mature' students at Christ For The Nations (CFNI) School of Worship. In the years that followed we maintained our friendship and now serve together in training worshippers at CFNI.

My friend, Alan, has a burning desire to see true worship released in the Earth. This book will challenge and encourage you to be the worshippers that God is looking for. As you digest the material in '*Becoming Worship*,' prepare to be changed; then pass on the insights to others!

Thank you, Alan, for this wonderful book!

Simon Dunn
CFNI Worship Major Director
Antioch Church Worship Pastor

DEDICATION

I dedicate this book to my best friend, my wife
and the love of my life, Wanessa Bathke Carvalho.

ACKNOWLEDGMENTS

Thank you, Wanessa, for marrying me and for letting God shine His Love through your Life. Without your love, support, strength, trust and patience, this book would be nothing but empty pages.

Thank you, Mom, for showing me what AUTHENTIC WORSHIP looks like when nobody is watching us.

Thank you, Dad, for showing me how to trust the Lord by example.

Thank you, Rachael Streifel, for believing in what I had to write and for helping me make this book become a reality.

Thank you, Christ For The Nations Institute for shaping my Worship Theology.

TABLE OF CONTENTS

INTRODUCTION

The purpose of this book is to help us grow toward our real identity in both our private and cooperative worship lives. We are part of a culture that has an identity crisis. Our culture embraces the fact that what we do speaks louder than who we really are. Have you noticed that when people introduce someone, they share what they do and not who they really are? You will probably never hear, "This is Carl, a lovely father, good husband, hard working man of integrity, who is committed to the Lord, his family and his church."

Instead, the first question is always, "What do you do?" How would you describe yourself if someone was to ask, "Who are you?" instead of "What do you do?" Our society is all about appearances, success and talent. It's not about who we are anymore. Receiving recognition from people seems to be more important than receiving recognition from God! Our title,

> **HOW WOULD YOU DESCRIBE YOURSELF IF SOMEONE ASKED, "WHO ARE YOU," INSTEAD OF "WHAT DO YOU DO?"**

position, talent, appearance and bloodline will stamp an acceptance pass right on our foreheads.

In the Book of Romans, Paul appeals to the Church of Rome to not be conformed by the way the kingdom of darkness thinks. He urges the Church to change their hearts and offer their lives as true and proper worship, so they could see God's perfect will for their lives.

> "Therefore, I urge you, brothers and sisters, in view of God's mercy, to offer your bodies as a living sacrifice, holy and pleasing to God—this is your true and proper worship. Do not conform to the pattern of this world, but be transformed by the renewing of your mind. Then you will be able to test and approve what God's will is—his good, pleasing and perfect will" (Romans 12:1, 2).

The moment our worship lives start depending upon our position, our title or our human recognition, we will find ourselves in a deep identity crisis. Our position and title won't change who we are on the inside!

Before we do what we are supposed to do, we need to be what God has called us to be! That's how what we do, becomes something powerful in the Kingdom of God!

No matter what we do in life or what we love the most, we all have a calling and a purpose as worshippers. Before you begin Chapter One, think about the following questions:

- What would happen if we became a generation of worshippers who knew who we were in Christ?
- What would happen if we became worshippers who knew how to worship God both corporately and privately?
- What would happen if we became a generation of worshippers who were not ashamed of expressing their gratitude and love to God?
- What would happen if we became a generation of worshippers who worshiped God above our own preferences and musical tastes?
- What would happen if we became a generation of worshippers who would be the expression of God's love?

The Church is in desperate need of authentic worshippers. This book was not written to help you become a better worship leader or a better musician. It was written to help you become a better worshipper. We need to constantly remind ourselves that our primary goal is not to lead worship, sing, or play our favorite instrument; it is to simply—**worship**.

God has called you to become something far greater than you could ever imagine. He has called you to become a living sacrifice.

"... Before we do what we are supposed to do, we need to be what God has called us to be! That's how what we do, becomes something powerful in the Kingdom of God ..."

Alanderson Carvalho

Chapter 1

A NEW IDENTITY

In the time of Jesus, what a person had and what they wore, would tell you who they were. A person's title and position would determine who they were. Jesus came and established a new culture—a culture in which the inward was more important than the outward.

Today's society is not very different from Jesus' time. People still value people for what they do or have. All we have to do is turn on the TV, engage in social activities or social media and we will see this reality in every part of society; sometimes, even among believers.

Recalling King David's story, he went to school to learn Jewish literature like every other boy his age, but in his father's eyes he didn't have the potential to become a great leader. One day, he was in the field taking care of his father's sheep when Samuel the prophet came to his father's house bringing an instruction from the Lord.

"Jesse had seven of his sons pass before Samuel, but Samuel said to him, 'The LORD has not chosen these.' So he asked Jesse, 'Are these all the sons you have?' 'There is still the youngest,' Jesse answered. 'He is tending the sheep.' Samuel said, 'Send for him; we will not sit down until he arrives.' So he sent for him and had him brought in ... Then the LORD said, 'Rise and anoint him; this is the one.' So Samuel took the horn of oil and anointed him in the presence of his brothers, and from that day on the Spirit of the LORD came powerfully upon David" (1 Samuel 16:10-13).

BEFORE DAVID BECAME A PROPHET, A PRIEST, A KING AND THE SONGWRITER OF HIS TIME, HE WAS A WORSHIPPER!

In that very moment, he faced an unexpected call on his life. He stood out among his other seven brothers to become, not only a great king, but a king who would bring a new order of worship to his people. It was a big surprise, especially to his father. Before David became a prophet, a priest, a king and the songwriter of his time, he was a worshipper! He started out as a worshipper, who took care of his dad's sheep, and his heart caught God's attention. God called David when he was watching sheep! While he was just a shepherd boy, he found his identity in God.

He became one of the most recognized names in the Bible, conquering titles and positions of honor. In the eyes of the people, he was not the shepherd anymore; he was the rich, conqueror and powerful King David. In the eyes of God, He was still the same David from the shepherding days; he was still a man after God's own heart. So, who are we in God's eyes?

IN HIS PRESENCE

Many people in our churches haven't found their new identity as worshippers yet. Day in and day out they do what they are supposed to do, but they haven't become what they are supposed to be! This identity crisis holds us back from being used to our full potential and to experience the fullness of God in our worship lives. Finding our real identity in God's presence won't make us perfect or spiritual super heroes, but it will open our spiritual eyes to see Who our God truly is and how we can be transformed in our worship lives.

When I started my journey in music ministry, I was just twelve years old. In my mind, I was about to become JUST A DRUMMER. I still remember my teacher picking me up once a week and taking me to the church where he taught drums. Soon, I was playing almost every Sunday morning. I loved to play, and the only reason I was excited to go to church was because I was in love with the drums.

A few years later, before I moved to the United States, I started to learn my second instrument, the acoustic guitar. I began without any pretension, but I ended up falling in love with the new sound that I was able to create with my own hands. I had discovered a new world of music with chords and notes that changed my life forever. I still remember that incredible moment when I played my first song. Once again, I found myself in love with the music and saw myself as just a musician.

Many of us go through the same identity crisis that I went through many years ago. Some find their identity in the past; others find their identity in what they love to do. Others find their identity in their messed-up, family background, but who are we, truly?

I asked this question over and over when I found out that I was adopted and that my aunt was actually my biological mother. When I received the news, I saw my whole identity disappear right in front of me. I spent the next few years of my life wondering who my biological father was, and not knowing who he was, made me feel like I didn't know who I was. Therefore, my identity was not clear—with my HUMAN eyes at least.

In the late 90s, we moved to the United States, and in a blink of an eye, I found myself working two, and sometimes three jobs to help my family. I was the older son in a family of six people. I was also the only one with enough English to order a burger at McDonald's.

Everything was new for me. I had to learn a new language,

make new friends, meet new people, embrace a new culture and soon I would be discovering my new identity in my Heavenly Father. Within those days of so many questions and so much uncertainty, I started to develop a new relationship with God; and in His presence, I started to see what I could not see before. I started to see my real identity in Christ as a worshipper. I made myself available to become the person God intended for me to be.

During one of those hard winters in New York, I found myself in my room praying to God. I was asking Him for direction in my life. Suddenly, I experienced something that I'd never experienced before with that intensity; I experienced God's presence. In a matter of seconds, a great desire to know Him took over my heart, and for the first time in years, I wanted more than to just play music. For many years, I helped my dad in the worship ministry at our church, and people knew me as "the pastor's son." This title wasn't always easy to carry, as the expectations were always very high. I've also seen the hardship in ministry that could have made me not want to be a part of ministry, ever! But when I faced God's unexpected call in my life, there was nothing I could do to turn it down.

The moment I renewed my mind and let God change my heart, I was able to see my real purpose in life and who I was supposed to become. Who I really was became clear right before my very eyes. I didn't have the "theological word" for what I was feeling, but I knew I was supposed to be more than just a singer or a musician.

"I will give you a new heart and put a new spirit in you; I will remove from you your heart of stone and give you a heart of flesh" (Ezekiel 36:26).

> **AT THE MOMENT MY HEART CHANGED, WHO I WAS ALSO CHANGED. THEN, MY MOTIVES CHANGED, AND MY LIFE ALSO CHANGED.**

I understood that worship was about who or what our hearts belonged to. At the moment my heart changed, who I was also changed. Then, my motives changed, and my life also changed.

We all need to advance in our spiritual life, and the only way to achieve this is by discovering who we are in His presence. Having an authentic worship life will change the way we live our lives. It will change our churches and our relationships. It will produce spiritual and physical healing. It will give us a new identity. All these changes will take place after we believe and begin to work toward the person God intends for us to be.

"Therefore, if anyone is in Christ, the new creation has come: The old has gone, the new is here!" (2 Corinthians 5:17).

I could have chosen to feel rejected, lost, and insecure, but instead, I decided to believe, receive, and become. The enemy is always trying to sow these feelings back into our hearts, and we need to continue to come back into His Word in His presence.

Coming into God's presence was not only my starting point, but also my place of transformation and growth. Twenty years later, I find myself going back to that same place of growth and transformation—His presence.

I realized that coming into His presence was a necessity, if I wanted to continue to grow in my new identity in Christ.

In the Book of Exodus, we see God's people missing their great opportunity to be completely changed by the presence of God. When God delivered His people out of slavery into Egypt, he called Moses and made a marriage proposal to them by saying:

> "Now if you obey me fully and keep my covenant,
> then out of all nations you will be my treasured
> possession" (Exodus 19:5).

When Moses told the people about God's proposal, the people said yes and God asked Moses to meet His people at the foot of Mount Sinai. The expectation was probably overwhelming, as they would meet the God Who brought them out of darkness for the first time. But something didn't happen according to the plan. A day that was supposed to be a day of intimacy between God and his people, turned out to be a fiasco.

When God approached the people, a thick cloud covered the mountain and a very loud trumpet blasted. There was lightning and thunder everywhere, as the Bridegroom was ready to encounter His bride, but the bride ran away in fear of His presence.

The people said to Moses,

> "... Speak to us yourself and we will listen. But do not have God speak to us or we will die" (Exodus 20:19).

Because His people didn't want to meet Him face to face, God had to change the original plan and come up with a different plan—build an Ark to rest His presence upon and to establish the priests.

Isn't it amazing that God was trying everything to be in the midst of His people? It's so amazing that God still wants to have a great relationship with all of His children, but even today, people still want to ask a holy man to go and talk to God and bring something for them because they don't want to meet God for themselves?

Very often people are overtaken by the fear of commitment. Our Worship lives are nothing more than being able to commit ourselves to the One Who keeps pursuing us.

Because of this fear of Commitment, God then chose only the tribe of Levi to be the priests to carry the Ark of the Covenant. (The very presence of God here on Earth). They stood before the Lord in worship and blessed the people in His name.

The good news is that in our new covenant in Christ, God has chosen us, the Church, to be His priests, and to experience His presence and bless others. Today, we can boldly go into the throne room of grace because of this covenant.

"But you are a chosen people, a royal priesthood, a holy nation, God's special possession, that you may declare the praises of Him who called you out of darkness into his wonderful light" (1 Peter 2:9).

QUESTIONS FOR REFLECTION

1. What are the different ways you can experience transformation in God's presence besides Sunday mornings?

_____

_____

_____

_____

2. According to Chapter One, what is God's greatest desire?

_____

_____

_____

_____

3. Explain with your own words the phrase: "Before we do what we are supposed to do, we need to be what God has called us to be!"

_____

_____

_____

_____

Chapter 2

COME IN TO BE CHANGED—COME OUT TO BLESS

The Hebrew word for priest is *Kohen*, which means, "come in, come out." Come in to God's presence and come out to bless the people. The biblical Hebrew context for worship, in the priest's life, was to study in transformation. No matter who we are or what we do, our primary responsibility is to *Come* into worship to be changed, and *Come* out to live what we have experienced and learned from God to bless the people around us.

That's the only way we will be able to carry His presence and bless the people. We often miss the opportunity to point people to Christ because our life is not reflecting the Jesus that we are preaching or teaching about. Frequently, people connect each other by their personalities, personal stories, talents, ideas and doctrine, instead of connecting them with Christ.

Our job description is not to hit that high note or perform an outstanding guitar solo, but to reflect Jesus in everything we do. As priests, we should not only be carrying God's presence, but also be blessing everyone around us.

Sometimes we say things because it sounds good. A few examples are, "I'll pray for you," or "I love you," or "God bless you." But are we really praying for them? Do we really love them? Are we really blessing them?

As a priest, we should be doing all of the above. People won't remember the last song we sang, but they will remember when we pray for their sick child. They won't remember our beautiful voices, but they will remember when we give our time to listen to them. They won't remember last week's set list, but they will remember when we meet their needs. They will remember us for blessing their lives.

Being a church that is full of priests is God's dream for every church! It's our responsibility, as a new creature in Christ, to carry His presence and to help people see the God we know, bringing them closer to Him, not only Sunday mornings, but also everywhere we go.

Everywhere we go people will have the opportunity to meet with God, if we let God change our lives in His presence. In God's plan of redemption, the church is called to be priests who will reach out to everyone around us.

Experiencing God's presence comes before anyone can carry His presence. Before carrying His presence, we need to experience His truth, transformation, love and power that are found only in Him. I want to help you understand why experiencing God's presence is vital in our lives as worshippers.

> **WE WANT TO CLAIM VICTORY, NOT BECAUSE OF THE NOISE OF OUR MUSIC, BUT BECAUSE WE HAVE A REAL RELATIONSHIP WITH GOD.**

Since the exit from Egypt, the people of Israel had been decaying spiritually. As people started to worship false gods and do what pleased them, immorality and evil began to rise again in the midst of the people of Israel. God's hand was reaching out to them, but they decided to turn and walk the other way.

They went to war against the Philistines, shouting as if the victory was theirs because they thought they were carrying God's presence, but their shout was empty before God. It was just noise. We want to claim victory—not because of the noise of our music—but because we have a real relationship with God. That's the only thing keeping us away from losing the most important thing in our lives—God's presence.

Israel lost the Ark of the Covenant because of their lack of a relationship with God. When they lost the presence of God, they lost the only thing that gave them identity. Eli allowed the armies of Israel to take the Ark of the Covenant and use it as a lucky charm to force God to defeat the Philistines.

Without His transformation, we can't carry His presence.

Without His presence, there's no point in doing whatever it is we are trying to do in His Name. We should not rely on our own understanding, but on God's presence at all times, with or without an outstanding, full band, or just an acoustic guitar, and with or without cool media resources or good sound. If His presence does not go with us, we do what we do in vain.

People will forget our songs, our speech, our preaching, but they will never forget the experience of having God's presence in their midst. His habitation is the only thing that differentiates us from all other organizations. No matter how jumpy and noisy we can get on Sunday mornings, how many talented people we have on our team, or how prepared we are, without God's presence, we are just empty noise—just a bunch of people lost in the wilderness!

In Exodus, we see God calling His people stiffed-necked! A stiff-necked person is not someone who is in need of a chiropractor, but someone who is extremely stubborn, wanting things their own way, not listening, not understanding, and in some cases, not even listening to God. God was so disappointed in them that He offered to send an angel on their journey to the Promised Land, instead of going Himself. Moses quickly replied to God.

> "If your Presence does not go with us, do not send
> us up from here" (Exodus 33:15).

Moses clearly understood how important it was to have God's presence with them at all times!

No matter what we do in lighting, video, sound and stage, we want people to leave our service knowing that God spoke to the people ... to THEIR heart. We want them to clap, not because they loved the music, but because God's glory was so intense that they couldn't contain themselves! We want them to experience the living presence of God.

WE ARE MINISTERS

Once we experience His presence and transformation, we become not only priests of the new covenant, but we become Ministers of the new covenant!

"Not that we are competent in ourselves to claim anything for ourselves, but our competence comes from God. He has made us competent as ministers of a new covenant—not of the letter but of the Spirit; for the letter kills, but the Spirit gives life." (2 Corinthians 3:5, 6).

Unfortunately, being a minister of the new covenant has become something exclusive of pastors, evangelists and missionaries. Paul saw the Church as a community of ministers when he explains the function of the body of Christ.

"So Christ himself gave the apostles, the prophets, the evangelists, the pastors and teachers, to equip his people for works of service, so that the body of Christ may be built up until we all reach unity in the faith and in the knowledge of the Son of God and become mature, attaining to the whole measure of the fullness of Christ. Then we will no longer be infants, tossed back and forth by the waves, and blown here and there by every wind of teaching and by the cunning and craftiness of people in their deceitful scheming. Instead, speaking the truth in love, we will grow to become in every respect the mature body of him who is the head, that is, Christ. From him the whole body, joined and held together by every supporting ligament, grows and builds itself up in love, as each part does its work." (Ephesians 4:11-16).

Our primary calling is to declare God's great acts and marvelous wonders. It is not to self-promote our complex phases of impact on social media. Our primary calling is to be ministers of His new covenant.

"The Spirit of the LORD is upon me, for He has anointed me to bring Good News to the poor. He has sent me to proclaim that captives will be released, that the blind will see, that the oppressed will be set free ..." (Luke 4:18, NLT).

There's something more than just receiving all of God's benefits and waiting for the second coming of the Lord. Many churchgoers are adhering to what I call "The Walmart Effect."

People go to Walmart because they want to buy the same product other stores have for 30% less. The same thing happens in our churches when we adhere to this way of being. Many times, the goal of the people is to receive the best message, the best music, the best nursery, the best sound system, the best seats, the best stage, the best lighting system, the best lobby, the best coffee shop, the best musicians, and in return, we give very little—many times, giving almost NOTHING.

This is not about giving money; this is about being the ministers God intended us to be. Our Sunday mornings are very important in reaching people, but they are not the most important aspect of the Church. Remember, this is the place we come to be in His presence and experience Him before we go out to bless people. That's when we put our worship life to the test, when our job is to represent Him outside of the four walls of our church.

"We" the ministers of His new covenant are supposed to be the Church, whether we are in vocational ministry, paid staff or selling donuts.

The eighty minutes worth of Sunday service is not the defining point of what we do. There's nothing wrong with a great service with all the bells and whistles; but more than a perfect service, we are supposed to be functioning as ministers.

Corporate and private worship is powerful when we understand our calling as ministers. As ministers, our mission here on Earth is to be the expression of God's love—to proclaim hope, justice, peace, freedom, righteousness and the King's victory over sin and death on the cross.

Unfortunately, in history, we see people's attention deviate from these important aspects of God's Kingdom, when we let our personal inclinations emphasize the wrong aspects. Our calling as ministers is not to establish our own Christian earthly kingdom, but to proclaim His Kingdom where Christ is reigning in Glory.

Jesus had a hard time making people understand that His Kingdom was not of this world. Unfortunately, many still don't get it. A church can become the elite of the world, have all the financial and human resources and still not advance God's Kingdom, especially if it's not rooted in the message of Jesus Christ.

> **A CHURCH CAN BECOME THE ELITE OF THE WORLD, HAVE ALL THE FINANCIAL AND HUMAN RESOURCES AND STILL NOT ADVANCE GOD'S KINGDOM, ESPECIALLY IF IT'S NOT ROOTED IN THE MESSAGE OF JESUS CHRIST.**

After Jesus' death on the cross and His resurrection, the church grew rapidly under persecution when they had nothing, yet they had everything—the Holy Spirit revealing their new identity and a real perspective of God's Kingdom.

As ministers, we all need to understand that the Kingdom of God is only working dynamically when it's active in the person of Jesus Christ in our hearts. Our job as ministers is to release the true message of the Kingdom of God, which is not based on prosperity, political power, influence, emotional frenzy or religion. The Kingdom of God is manifested through His righteousness, peace and joy in our lives.

"For the Kingdom of God is not a matter of eating and drinking, but of righteousness, peace and joy in the Holy Spirit, because anyone who serves Christ in this way is pleasing to God and receives human approval" (Romans 14:17, 18).

"A psalm of praise. Of David. 'I will exalt You, my God the King; I will praise Your name forever and ever. Every day I will praise You and extol Your name forever and ever. Great is the LORD and most worthy of praise; His greatness no one can fathom. One generation commends Your works to another; they tell of Your mighty acts. They speak of the glorious splendor of Your majesty—and I will meditate on Your wonderful works. They tell of the power of Your awesome works and I will proclaim Your great deeds. They celebrate Your abundant goodness and joyfully sing of Your righteousness. The LORD is gracious and compassionate; slow to anger and rich in love. The LORD is good to all; he has compassion on all he has made. All Your works praise You, LORD; Your faithful people extol You. They tell of the glory of Your kingdom and speak of Your might, so that all people may know of Your mighty acts and the glorious splendor of Your kingdom. Your kingdom is an everlasting kingdom, and Your dominion endures through all generations. The LORD is trustworthy in all He promises and faithful in all he does. The LORD upholds all who fall and lifts up all who are bowed down. The eyes of all look to you, and you give them their food at the proper time. You open your hand and satisfy the desires of every living thing. The LORD is righteous in all His ways and faithful in all He does. The LORD is near to all who call on Him, to all who call on Him in truth. He fulfills the desires of those who fear Him; He hears their cry and saves them. The Lord watches over all who love Him, but all the wicked He will destroy. My mouth will speak in praise of the LORD. Let every creature praise His holy name forever and ever'" (Psalm 145:1-21).

TAKING THE FORM OF A SERVANT

We always associate the word Minister with the clergy or the head of a government department, but in this new identity in Christ, serving others became the essence of the word "minister" or "ministry." The moment we experience God in our lives we become servants. David found himself doing something that had nothing to do with music—shepherding. He also found himself defeating one of the greatest enemies of Israel, while he was serving.

On an ordinary day, David was asked to take lunch to his brothers. They were on the battlefield, camping along the

Valley of Elah, with the other soldiers for days. They were in a tense cold war between the Philistines and the Israelites. For forty days, Goliath threw words of fear over the people of God. Goliath brought intimidation to the people of God and where there is no confidence, there is no worship. David was only a delivery boy when he faced this situation and God used him to prove that He is greater and higher than any enemy or giant. David trusted the God he served and took back everything that belonged to the people of God, so they could begin to bear fruit again!

Being a servant seems to be a forgotten qualification in our contemporary leadership model. We want people to serve, but many times, we minimize our serving time by reserving our servanthood to Sunday mornings.

The Apostle Paul, after experiencing Jesus Christ on his way to Damascus, realized that he was not the person he thought he was. In a matter of seconds, his identity was changed by the powerful presence of Jesus and he became a servant.

"Paul, a servant of Christ Jesus, called to be an apostle and set apart for the gospel of God —" (Romans 1:1).

Yes, he was an apostle, but mainly, he was a servant. For some of the disciples, it took a long time for them to get it, and in Mark 9:33 we see the evidence of this:

"They came to Capernaum. When he was in the house, he asked them, 'What were you arguing about on the road?' But they kept quiet because on the way they had argued about who was the greatest. Sitting down, Jesus called the Twelve and said, 'Anyone who wants to be first must be the very last, and the servant of all'" (Mark 9:33-35).

Somewhere along the way, we lost the whole idea of being a servant. Servanthood and humbleness do not seem very appealing to some of the modern teachings. No matter how cool your title or your position, you will only become great in the Kingdom of God, when you become a servant. The best leaders are people who are servants to play, sing, preach or lead, but they are also available to vacuum the church if needed. The best leaders are people who love, serve and care for the people they are ministering to.

> **YOU MAY FIND YOURSELF MOVING UP THE LADDER, BUT THE HIGHER YOU GO, THE MORE YOU SHOULD SERVE.**

The "worldly" corporate model teaches something completely different from Jesus' servant model. The primarily goal of the worldly system is to do whatever it takes to climb the ladder. You will step over people and fight hard for your way to the top to make sure you get to a place where you will have the whole world serving you. In Jesus' model, every promotion is downward. You may be finding yourself moving up the ladder but the higher you go, the more humble you need to become, and the more you should serve.

SERVANTHOOD AND HUMBLENESS

"Instead, whoever wants to become great among you must be your servant, and whoever wants to be first must be your slave—just as the Son of Man did not come to be served, but to serve, and to give His life as a ransom for many" (Matthew 20:26-28).

The greatest man who ever walked on Earth, Jesus, is the perfect example of a great servant. He dropped the form of God and took on the form of a servant, as Jesus, the Galilean preacher from Nazareth. He laid down His life, even though He was God! If we want to find our identity in worship, we need to do the same.

"In your relationships with one another, have the same mindset as Christ Jesus: Who, being in very nature God, did not consider equality with God something to be used to his own advantage; rather,

He made Himself nothing by taking the very nature of a servant, being made in human likeness. And being found in appearance as a man, He humbled Himself by becoming obedient to death—even death on a cross!" (Philippians 2:5-8).

QUESTIONS FOR REFLECTION

1. According to the godly, priestly order, how can you bless others?

_____

_____

_____

_____

2. What was the one thing Moses prioritized in the wilderness, and how can we do the same?

_____

_____

_____

_____

3. What is our primary calling as Ministers?

_____

_____

_____

_____

4. How can you describe the difference between man's kingdom and God's Kingdom?

_____

_____

_____

_____

5. How can you become a better servant?

_____

_____

_____

_____

Chapter 3

LOVE AND WORSHIP

WE ARE LOVED

The starting point toward our new *Identity* is knowing and receiving God's Love. Most of our songs and the Church's vision statements have the word LOVE in them. You can't go wrong with the word love. Love is the foundation of all our Christian beliefs. We all know that, as Christians, we are supposed to love; but what many of us don't know is how to BE LOVED. Have you noticed that not everyone knows how to act when we express love to them? Some people even get all stiff when we hug them. Others don't know what to say or how to react. When actions of love come our way, sometimes because of our different backgrounds, cultures and personalities, we don't know how to act.

In God's presence, not only have I found my identity, but the Father has made me realize how special we are to Him. I know, without a shadow of a doubt, that I am one of His favorite people on this Earth. When I say that, I don't mean that He loves me more than He loves others, but somehow, I feel like I have a special place in His heart. Frankly, that's the way we all should feel about our Heavenly Father's love for us.

We need to stop looking for acceptance in the wrong places and with the wrong people. When the Father looks at us, by the blood of His Son, He sees the beauty and perfection that is in each one of us.

Before we start singing, preaching or saying anything about His love, we need to have the ability to receive His love for us. We love because he first loved us. (1 John 4:19).

The understanding that *we are loved* is the first step in being able to Love God and people. There's an old hymn that I love to sing because it's the truth of God. The chorus says,

"How deep the Father's love for us,
how vast beyond all measure ..."

We should accept the fact that our Heavenly Father loves us beyond all measure. This is the starting place, so we can begin to reflect His love to the world.

"See what kind of love the Father has given to us that we should be called children of God; and so we are. The reason why the world does not know us is that it did not know him" (1 John 3:1, ESV).

"The LORD your God is in your midst, a mighty one who will save; he will rejoice over you with gladness; he will quiet you by his love; he will exult over you with loud singing" (Zephaniah 3:17, ESV).

God is calling you to experience His love through your life and to become a new person. I urge you to receive this love in your life, so that you may be able to understand who you are in Him.

LOVING GOD

One of the most important Jewish texts in the Bible is found in Deuteronomy 6:4-9, where God sets the foundation of their worship lives under a new commitment.

"Listen, O Israel! The LORD is our God, the LORD alone. And you must love the LORD your God with all your **heart**, all your **soul**, and all your **strength**. And you must commit yourselves wholeheartedly to these commands that I am giving you today. Repeat them again and again to your children. Talk about them when you are at home and when you are on the road, when you are going to bed and when you are getting up. Tie them to your hands and wear them on your forehead as reminders. Write them on the doorposts of your house and on your gates" (Deuteronomy 6:4-9, NLT).

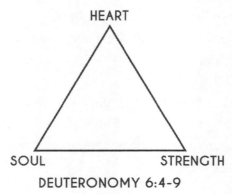

DEUTERONOMY 6:4-9

Here we find for the first time a kind of worship triad where God is instructing His children on what worship should look like from that point on. Clearly, God is showing that real worship is about loving HIM with all that we are and all that we have.

In the New Testament God shows us through Jesus' ministry this "worship triad" once again. This is when the Pharisees and Sadducees try to embarrass Jesus in front of a crowd during one of his teachings.

"'Teacher, which is the greatest commandment in the Law?' Jesus replied: 'Love the Lord your God with all your heart and with all your soul and with all your mind.' This is the first and greatest commandment. And the second is like it: 'Love your neighbor as yourself.' All the Law and the Prophets hang on these two commandments" (Matthew 22:36-40).

Out of this "triad" we find not only the most important teaching of Jesus, but also the center of Jesus' teaching. Loving the Lord with all that we are—our thinking, using our strength, talents, and gifts, and giving all that we have. If what we do is really worship, we should be experiencing this triad in our lives.

IF WHAT WE DO IS REALLY WORSHIP, WE SHOULD BE EXPERIENCING THE "TRANSFORMATION TRIAD" IN OUR LIVES.

Jesus then added something that would once and for all change the world's mentality. He commanded us to love people.

"And the second is like it: 'Love your neighbor as yourself.' All the Law and the Prophets hang on these two commandments" (Matthew 22:39, 40).

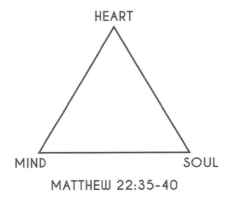

MATTHEW 22:35-40

47

LOVING PEOPLE

Loving people is a command from Jesus; and many times we neglect this part of the commandment. One time, during an interview for a worship pastor position, after meeting all my requirements for the job description, the pastor asked me a final question that would seal the deal. He asked, "Do you have people skills? Are you a people person?"

This pastor understood how important relational skills were in ministry. I strongly believe that we were created to connect with people in fellowship, witnessing God's grace and love. We can't be the Church or even be in ministry if we are unable to have healthy relationships with people! No matter how hard it is to relate to people, we need to do our part, and there is only one way to maintain a good relationship with people—loving them the way the Bible instructs us to love.

We can sing, write books, lead worship, be on TV and look very spiritual, but without love, our worship is a forgery.

"If I speak in the tongues of men or of angels, but do not have love, I am only a resounding gong or a clanging cymbal. If I have the gift of prophecy and can fathom all mysteries and all knowledge, and if I have a faith that can move mountains, but do not have love, I am nothing. If I give all I possess to the poor and give over my body to hardship that I may boast, but do not have love, I gain nothing" (1 Corinthians 13:1-3).

Loving those around us is a choice. Hollywood tells us that we should do what we feel like doing, and then, what we feel will turn into love. The Bible tells us that love is not a feeling. Love is a decision—a commandment. Your decisions will bring forth your emotions. If we really want to obey Jesus' command to Love, we need to know how to love unconditionally. That means loving all kinds of people— people with different beliefs, habits, priorities, cultures, etc. God wants us to love the people around us because His love never fails.

John was known as the beloved disciple. He understood that LOVE holds everything together in the Kingdom of God; and in many of his writings he reminds people that love is the most important commandment.

When John was the pastor of a church in Ephesus, the Emperor Domitian exiled him, sending Him to an island called Patmos. Domitian saw John as a threat to his rule. During his exile years, John wrote the Book of Revelation and years later, when released from exile, he returned to his church in Ephesus.

Historians tell us that by this time, he was a very old man and nobody recognized him. As he sat in the back row of his own church, people started to question, "Who is the man seated in the last row? A few minutes later, someone shouted with excitement, 'It's John!'" They all circled around him asking questions. After all, he was the last person on Earth that walked with Jesus. All the other disciples had already died.

People asked him all kinds of questions about Jesus and His teachings. They kept on going until someone said, "Stop it! Let the man say something! Go ahead John. Say something." John walked to the front of the church, looked at the crowd and said, "Little children, love one another!" If we have a misconception about love, then we also have a misconception about God. If we don't understand love, then we don't understand God—because God IS love.

> "Dear friends, let us love one another, for love comes from God. Everyone who loves has been born of God and knows God. Whoever does not love does not know God, because God is love. This is how God showed his love among us: He sent his one and only Son into the world that we might live through him. This is love: not that we loved God, but that he loved us and sent his Son as an atoning sacrifice for our sins. Dear friends, since God so loved us, we also ought to love one another. No one has ever seen God; but if we love one another, God lives in us and his love is made complete in us. This is how we know that we live in him and he in us: He has given us of his Spirit. And we have seen and testify that the Father has sent his Son to be the Savior of the world. If anyone acknowledges that Jesus is the Son of God, God lives in them and they in God. And so we know and rely on the love God has for us. God is love. Whoever lives in love lives in God, and God in them. This is how love is made complete among us so that we will have confidence on the

Day of Judgment: In this world we are like Jesus. There is no fear in love. But perfect love drives out fear, because fear has to do with punishment. The one who fears is not made perfect in love. We love because he first loved us. Whoever claims to love God yet hates a brother or sister is a liar. For whoever does not love their brother and sister, whom they have seen, cannot love God, whom they have not seen" (1 John 4:7-20).

According to Jesus, loving God and people is the greatest command in the Bible. John says that it's impossible to love God and not love people. So, why do people still neglect such an important command?

"'Teacher, which is the most important commandment in the law of Moses?' Jesus replied, 'You must love the Lord your God with all your heart, all your soul, and all your mind.' This is the first and greatest commandment. A second is equally important: 'Love your neighbor as yourself.' The entire law and all the demands of the prophets are based on these two commandments." (Matthew 22:36-40, NLT).

When I look at my matrimonial life, I am able to understand what the Bible is trying to explain about love. Our wedding was not exactly the way we had intended it to be, but I will never forget the moment my gorgeous bride walked into that chapel on that beautiful spring afternoon. My legs were trembling, and my heart felt like it was going to jump out of my chest! For a few seconds, I felt like the world had stopped moving.

After that unique and special moment, all that I remember is the usual wedding ceremony program—the ring bearer crying before entering the church and a family member being dramatic before, during and after the ceremony!

What made our wedding a special event was not the violin playing during the ceremony, the DJ playing the coolest Christian dance hits, or even the Dulce de Leche cake filling. It was the love we had for one another. Love not only made our day a special day, but it has made our entire journey together special.

Couples spend months planning a two-hour event, and very often they forget to put the same kind of effort into their relationship as a married couple. All couples make the same promises to one another during their marriage vows. Most of them will experience the same traditional wedding ceremony, and yet, half of them will end up in divorce court. The same thing can happen to us as worshippers. Many people see their worship lives as just an event or a single act.

How many people spend time planning the perfect worship or preaching "event" without love? Without love, everything we do will be just an event without any spiritual meaning.

In 1 Corinthians, Paul warns us by saying that without love, everything we do has no meaning.

"If I could speak all the languages of earth and of angels, but didn't love others, I would only be a noisy gong or a clanging cymbal. If I had the gift of prophecy, and if I understood all of God's secret plans and possessed all knowledge, and if I had such faith that I could move mountains, but didn't love others, I would be nothing" (1 Corinthians 13:1, 2, NLT).

Why do we do what we do? What is our motivation? If the answer is not love, we do all that we do in vain.

Without love, we sing, clap our hands, play, teach, preach and show up at our Sunday morning "events" in vain. Without love, all we make is noise. Any one of us can get caught up in the "business" of ministry without loving the way the Bible instructs us to. Everything we do is worthless if it's not enabled by love. Any sacrificial act of worship has no meaning if it's not empowered by love.

People have been living a life of events that apparently have a big spiritual meaning to them but it's nothing more than a clanging cymbal in God's ears.

When I look at my ten years of marriage, I realize that even

> WHEN I LOOK AT MY TEN YEARS OF MARRIAGE, I REALIZE THAT EVEN THOUGH OUR WEDDING WAS SPECIAL, THE MOST BEAUTIFUL MEMORIES I HAVE ARE NOT FROM OUR "PERFECT WEDDING DAY" BUT FROM OUR IMPERFECT DAYS AS A COUPLE IN CHRIST'S LOVE.

though our wedding was special, the most beautiful memories I have are not from our "perfect wedding day" but from our imperfect days as a couple in Christ's love.

Whatever you do, do it for the right reason. It's not because of money, obligation, tradition, ritual, envy, and pressure or for the desire to show off. We do it out of an authentic love. It's time for the body of Christ to glorify the Father in their relationships. It's time to love.

QUESTIONS FOR REFLECTION

1. How can you apply the triad found on chapter three in your worship life?

   _____

   _____

   _____

   _____

2. How can you improve the way you love God and people in your daily life?

   _____

   _____

   _____

   _____

3. How can you become the expression of God's love to the world?

_____

_____

_____

_____

Chapter 4

A NEW HEART

"I will give you a new heart and put a new spirit in you; I will remove from you your heart of stone and give you a heart of flesh" (Ezekiel 36:26).

Every day, our hearts beat about 100,000 times—sending 2,000 gallons of blood through our bodies. The heart has the very important job of keeping our blood flowing. Every function of every organ in our body depends entirely on what flows from our heart. No wonder the Bible uses the heart as a symbol of our emotional, intellectual and moral activities.

In our hearts we discover who we are. If our hearts were visible to people, people would be able to finally see who we truly are, instead of what we do. The word heart in the Bible occurs over one thousand times, which makes it the most common term used to explain the mind, the conscience and the motives of a person. The heart becomes the expression of the individual's character and thoughts.

> "Above all else, guard your <u>heart</u>, for everything you do flows from it" (Proverbs 4:23).

Everything means EVERYTHING!!! … Including our worship lives. People try to trace worship to their favorite music styles, abilities and generation, but worship is not and will never be a generational or a musical issue. Worship is a "heart" issue. Worship is, and always will be, about the heart!

Why is it that some people have such a hard time expressing an authentic worship life to a God Who changed their broken heart?—Maybe it's because they haven't allowed God to change their hearts completely. Our faces, actions, and feelings, in both private and corporate worship, should express a heart that is totally transformed by God. That's when worship becomes more than four songs on Sunday mornings.

> "I will give them an undivided heart and put a new spirit in them; I will remove from them their heart of stone and give them a heart of flesh" (Ezekiel 11:19).

Our relationship with God will change our hearts (who we are) as worshippers. Every single thing that we do comes from our heart! So what is YOUR heart full of? If everything that we do comes from our hearts, everything that we do, act or say will reflect our hearts, and surely it will determine the course of our lives.

Being a worshipper is not about praying a single prayer of repentance and then continuing to live our lives like nothing has changed. When God enters our hearts, EVERYTHING is changed. A new heart means a new spirit and motivation.

The Bible tells us the story of a cherub whose pride led him to rebel against God. Because of his corrupted heart, he was cast out of Heaven and an ongoing war began—a war that is still taking place right now, even as you are reading this. It's about worship. It's all about the heart.

We can see clearly Lucifer's corrupt heart in his five statements in Isaiah.

"... I will ascend to the heavens;
I will raise my throne
    above the stars of God;
I will sit enthroned on the mount of assembly,
    on the utmost heights of Mount Zaphon.
I will ascend above the tops of the clouds;
I will make myself like the Most High" (Isaiah 14:13, 14).

Lucifer was cast out of Heaven, and ever since then, he has been after the worship and the exaltation that belongs only to God. After Jesus was baptized, Satan tried to make even the Son of God worship him.

"Then Jesus was led by the Spirit into the wilderness to be tempted by the devil. After fasting forty days and forty nights, he was hungry. The tempter came to him and said, 'If you are the Son of God, tell these stones to become bread.' Jesus answered, 'It is written: 'Man shall not live on bread alone, but on every word that comes from the mouth of God.' Then the devil took him to the holy city and had him stand on the highest point of the temple. 'If you are the Son of God,' he said, 'throw yourself down.' For it is written: 'He will command his angels concerning you, and they will lift you up in their hands, so that you will not strike your foot against a stone.' Jesus answered him, 'It is also written: 'Do not put the Lord your God to the test.' Again, the devil took him to a very high mountain and showed him all the kingdoms of the world and their splendor. 'All this I will give you,' he said, 'if you will bow down and worship me.' Jesus said to him, 'Away from me, Satan!' For it is written: 'Worship the Lord your God, and serve him only.' Then the devil left him, and angels came and attended him" (Matthew 4:1-11).

The devil will try everything to get our attention, time, money, heart and even our worship. Throughout history, Lucifer has been deceiving people with his lies. There are people who worship everything and anything, except the glorious, ever-living God.

In the story of the golden calf in Exodus 32, the children of Israel had been in bondage in Egypt for over four hundred years. God called Moses, and told him that He had heard their cries and was going to deliver them (see Exodus 3:6–8).

God delivered His people from Egypt displaying His magnificent power and continued doing it during their journey. With over three million people under Moses' leadership, they found themselves not knowing where they were going—no army, no system, no religion, no wealth, no regulations and no land—just a promise.

That's when God called Moses to come up the mountain. He was going to give him what would be the beginning and the foundation of everything they needed—His Commandments. God met with Moses at the top of Mount Sinai to give him these valuable instructions for His people. While Moses was up on the mountain receiving God's Commandments, the people who were left down at the foot of the mountain, got impatient and insecure.

Moses spent forty days and forty nights on Mount Sinai (see Exodus 24:18), and the people started to make gods for themselves to follow and worship.

Aaron took their gold, which they had brought from Egypt, and melted it down to make a golden idol. Their hearts were still into

> OUR GOLDEN CALF COULD BE MONEY, POWER, POSITION, PEOPLE AND MORE. WE DON'T NEED TO WORSHIP SATAN TO MAKE HIM HAPPY. ALL WE HAVE TO DO IS DIVIDE OUR WORSHIP WITH ANY OTHER GOD.

pagan rituals and practices from Egypt, even after experiencing God's powers and miracles.

It is true that every person has the need to worship something. The human heart is always looking for something to worship. Our golden calf could be money, power, position, people and more. We don't need to worship Satan to make him happy. All we have to do is divide our worship with any other god. True worship is worshiping ONLY GOD.

> "You shall worship the Lord your God and Him only shall you serve" (Matthew 4:10, ESV).

If we worship God in spirit and in truth, we cannot worship anyone or anything else. Anything we worship, other than God, is an idol.

> "He who has clean hands and a pure heart, who does not lift up his soul what is false and does not swear deceitfully" (Psalm 24:4, ESV).

BE WISE AND GUARD YOUR HEART

We should always look into our heart and make sure that we keep it safe from the same spirit of pride that took over Lucifer's heart. Money, power and influence change people's hearts, and once these things change our hearts, we can't steward all the talent and the power that God has given to us. You probably know a lot of shocking stories about people who lost their wisdom because they did not guard their hearts during their journey.

"The fear of the LORD is the beginning of wisdom, and knowledge of the Holy One is understanding" (Proverbs 9:10).

For decades we have seen people misinterpreting the word "fear" in this passage. In Proverbs 9:10, "fear" doesn't represent an emotional fear only. As Westerners, we see it as something of the punitive nature. The Hebrew word for fear is *yirat Adonai*, which means love for God; walking with God; having a relationship with God; committing to God; Honor the Lord, obey the Lord. It's a covenant language!

Proverbs 9:10 ensures that a life of commitment, love, obedience and relationship with God is the beginning of a life of wisdom and knowledge. This relationship is exactly what the fear of God means in our lives. This covenant with God will bring honor to Him in a way that will impact our own lives. Out of this love for Him, we will submit our lives to worship God at all times.

Lucifer is one of the greatest examples in history of an individual using a lack of wisdom. His name in Hebrew is *Helel*, which comes from *Halal*. From this word, we have the word *Hallelujah,* which means to shine, to boast and to praise. His name alone gives us the certainty that he was an angel that shined God's glory.

However, his corrupt heart changed his purpose and history. He let pride and jealousy take over his heart, and he drifted away from his Source of light. When we look at Lucifer's example, we realize that God did not create evil. Evil is the result of our distance from God. Evil is the result of a self-sufficient, prideful and arrogant mentality. Evil is the result of the lack of *yirat* (fear) in our lives. The lack of light will result in darkness. The lack of goodness will result in evil.

According to Proverbs 9:10, the lack of *YIRAT* will turn us into dumb people. We can find many examples in the Bible of dumb people, who started out meaning well, but in time, stopped walking with God. Just like Lucifer, King Saul is a great example of this.

He was an ordinary boy who turned out very well. He was baptized in the Holy Spirit, was anointed and became the first King of Israel. He was a prophet and the Spirit of the Lord came upon him. He was the kind of leader who showed authority, and anyone would follow him in these days; but he was also eaten by jealousy and filled with arrogance and pride. A lack of wisdom brought Saul to a place of spiritual blindness. Saul had everything he needed to leave a great legacy, but instead, he was killed by his own sword.

If we have the mentality that this would never happen to us because we are the chosen and anointed ones, we should then be extra careful! We should keep cultivating our love for the Lord and continually walk in His ways. We should be listening and learning from Him and seek His presence in our lives at all times. That's how we become wise people.

> **SAUL HAD EVERYTHING HE NEEDED TO LEAVE A GREAT LEGACY, BUT INSTEAD, HE WAS KILLED BY HIS OWN SWORD.**

God's wisdom will help keep our hearts pure at all times, as our destiny could change because of the lack of it. The good news is that no matter how dark, lost or broken our hearts are, God is ready to restore and make it brand new. When King Hezekiah came to the throne of Judah, his priority was to restore the hearts of his people. His goal was to restore worship.

"... let us draw near to God with a sincere heart and with the full assurance that faith brings, having our hearts sprinkled to cleanse us from a guilty conscience and having our bodies washed with pure water" (Hebrews 10:22).

With the fall of the northern Kingdom, he probably had the opportunity to learn from their mistakes. A wise king always learns from his own mistakes, but a wiser king learns through someone else's mistakes. When Hezekiah became the king, he realized that the southern Kingdom could face the same destruction, if something was not done quickly. He started to do things that no other king had ever found the courage to do.

"In the first month of the first year of his reign, he opened the doors of the temple of the LORD and repaired them. He brought in the priests and the Levites, assembled them in the square on the east side and said: 'Listen to me, Levites! Consecrate yourselves now and consecrate the temple of the

LORD, the God of your ancestors. Remove all defilement from the sanctuary. Our parents were unfaithful; they did evil in the eyes of the LORD our God and forsook him. They turned their faces away from the LORD'S dwelling place and turned their backs on him. They also shut the doors of the portico and put out the lamps. They did not burn incense or present any burnt offerings at the sanctuary to the God of Israel. Therefore, the anger of the LORD has fallen on Judah and Jerusalem; he has made them an object of dread and horror and scorn, as you can see with your own eyes. This is why our fathers have fallen by the sword and why our sons and daughters and our wives are in captivity. Now I intend to make a covenant with the LORD, the God of Israel, so that his fierce anger will turn away from us. My sons, do not be negligent now, for the LORD has chosen you to stand before him and serve him, to minister before him and to burn incense'" (2 Chronicles 29:3-11).

After so many years of neglecting the temple and living in disobedience, the Levites finally said, "Yes" to the restoration and cleansing of their hearts. They consecrated themselves to the Lord, and they organized worship, according to God's direction and pattern again. A major restoration took place, and only after a major restructuring of worship was the assembly able to sing and play music that was acceptable to God.

"The whole assembly bowed in worship, while the musicians played and the trumpets sounded. All this continued until the sacrifice of the burnt offering was completed. When the offerings were finished, the king and everyone present with him knelt down and worshiped. King Hezekiah and his officials ordered the Levites to praise the LORD with the words of David and of Asaph the seer. So they sang praises with gladness and bowed down and worshiped" (2 Chronicles 29:28-30).

The purpose of the restoration of worship is clearly shown when King Hezekiah said,

"... You have now dedicated yourselves to the LORD. Come and bring sacrifices and thank offerings to the temple of the LORD' So the assembly brought sacrifices and thank offerings, and all whose hearts were willing brought burnt offerings." (2 Chronicles 29:31).

Now the real IDENTITY OF WORSHIP was finally restored, not only in the temple, but also in their hearts; the assembly was invited to come and bring their offering.

NOW THE REAL IDENTITY OF WORSHIP WAS FINALLY RESTORED, NOT ONLY IN THE TEMPLE, BUT ALSO IN THEIR HEARTS; THE ASSEMBLY WAS INVITED TO COME AND BRING THEIR OFFERING.

The Bible says that the change took place very quickly, as everyone played a part in this restoration. My heart is filled with hope by this amazing and powerful example of godly restoration. I know for sure we will be experiencing amazing things in our worship lives when we allow God to restore our hearts.

"Hezekiah and all the people rejoiced at what God had brought about for his people, because it was done so quickly" (2 Chronicles 29:36).

QUESTIONS FOR REFLECTION

1. How can you guard your heart?

_____

_____

_____

_____

2. What are the things in our society today that could represent a "Golden Calf" in our worship lives?

_____

_____

_____

_____

3. What do we need to restore first, in order to restore our worship and why?

_____

_____

_____

_____

Chapter 5

THE GLORY BELONGS TO GOD

If you are involved in worship music in any way, then you have probably noticed the growth of what I call idol-based-worship. The modern expression of worship and the growth of the "genre" made worship ministry in our churches become something popular and desired by many.

Unfortunately, because of these new developments in worship ministry, worship became questionable in many sectors of the contemporary church. This growth in the worship music blessed many with powerful worship lyrics that reached the four corners of the Earth, but this growth also brought a negative outcome, as many worshippers lost the real purpose of worship music.

What is considered a good worship song? Is it an anointed song, inspired by the Holy Spirit to bless and edify millions of people or a song that will sell millions of copies?

Every time God's Kingdom and the cross are used for personal profit, we take the same path Lucifer did. What is our motivation when being a part of any ministry? Are we really recording a CD because we want to bless lives or to merchandise God's glory? Is our priority to reflect God's love and power or to make a personal profit? Are our intentions and motivations free from iniquity? Are we really doing this out of a genuine calling from God to bless lives, or is it just another concert, another show, another gig, another way of showing off our abilities in the spot light?

Our primary job as Worship Leaders and songwriters is to minister to God and to bless the people. Selling the product should be only a consequence and not the primarily goal. We want people to experience God's habitation every time we sing our songs in our services, live recordings and also later in their homes when they press play on their iPods.

Even if we have the right motivation, my question would be: are our hearts prepared to receive the praises of the people around us? If we are good in what we do, we will probably receive many compliments in our lives, and no matter how good we are in what we do, receiving compliments can only become a problem when our hearts are not grounded in the likeness of Jesus.

Being a humble Christian doesn't mean that we have to deny

our talents and gifts, but we should have the conscience that everything we are and have is a gift from above. Isn't it amazing that Jesus, throughout the whole Bible, never brought the attention to Himself? He always brought people's attention to God the Father or the Holy Spirit. It's okay to recognize that we work hard and that we are talented; but this recognition should never produce in our hearts a proud eye.

... RECEIVING COMPLIMENTS CAN ONLY BECOME A PROBLEM WHEN OUR HEARTS ARE NOT GROUNDED IN THE LIKENESS OF JESUS.

When God gave David the victory over Goliath, He heard the crowd shouting,

> "Saul has slain his thousands, and David his tens of thousands" (1 Samuel 18:7).

Everybody gets recognized in life for something. These recognitions can cause people to become arrogant, and arrogance has no place in our worship. Neither does fake humility.

Many work hard to achieve recognition for their talents; it is possible to be recognized for all of our special gifts and still give all the glory to God, if we have our hearts grounded in Jesus.

> "For those who exalt themselves will be humbled, and those who humble themselves will be exalted" (Matthew 23:12).

On the flip side, we have idol-based-worshippers. We

recognize the idol-based syndrome when someone "famous" comes to lead worship in our churches. We show up expressing our praise and worship like we've done it before.

Idol-based-worshippers worship the person, the song, the album and the talent—NOT God. Their expectations rise when a famous guest comes to town, and we all know that our expectations should be in the One Who is available everywhere, every hour every minute—Jesus.

> **EVERYBODY GETS RECOGNIZED IN LIFE FOR SOMETHING. THESE RECOGNITIONS CAN CAUSE PEOPLE TO BECOME ARROGANT, AND ARROGANCE HAS NO PLACE IN OUR WORSHIP. NEITHER DOES FAKE HUMILITY.**

All throughout history, we see people worshiping the creation, instead of the Creator: stones, animals, stars and people!

The whole idea of idol based worship created a dependency in our worship lives. We need our favorite worship leader or band to worship; when this happens, we create a dependency, and we lose our identity as worshippers. God is not interested in worship that is fueled by idolatry. God is not interested in a worship that chooses mankind to be the ultimate mediator between God and man. The sad reality is that often people can't recognize that they are giving to man what belongs to the Father. There's a very thin line between idol-based-worshippers and authentic worshippers. Which side of this line are you on?

JEALOUSY AND COMPARISON

If the Glory belongs to God, why make comparisons? Why worry about asking the question: Who is the best? Who is the most famous? Who has the best voice? Who is the best preacher? Who makes more money? Who is more talented? With comparisons, we can easily become motivated by jealousy, turning our churches into coliseums of gladiators, if we don't watch our hearts. When we compete against each other, we defeat the purpose of God in our lives. We don't do our best because we are competing with people for recognition.

Jealousy of another person's fortune by comparison to our own misfortune is sin that invades our minds. Believing that another's blessing is causing our struggle or that someone else's promotion is our demotion is also jealousy. People that live in jealousy by comparison have two different perspectives.

1. They are better than anyone else; so they think: Why not me?
2. They have a victim MIND SET— "I am no good; I am a looser; I can't get what I want; it's your fault!"

Lucifer wasn't satisfied doing what he was created to do and jealousy and comparison changed the history of mankind.

"We do not dare to classify or compare ourselves with some who commend themselves. When they measure themselves by themselves and compare themselves with themselves, they are not wise" (2 Corinthians 10:12).

"A heart at peace gives life to the body, but envy rots the bones" (Proverbs 14:30).

"It is true that some preach Christ out of envy and rivalry, but others out of goodwill" (Philippians 1:15).

So what is the motivation of your heart? These are questions that we need to be honest with ourselves about because at the end of the day, we are the only ones, besides God, who can answer these questions.

When we become Worship we have a new perspective where everything we do is an opportunity to give God the Glory that belongs to Him!

QUESTIONS FOR REFLECTION

1. Describe with your own words the real purpose of worship music.

_____

_____

_____

_____

2. How can you avoid jealousy and comparison in your worship life?

_____

_____

_____

_____

3. Describe the results of an idol based worship congregation.

_____

_____

_____

_____

Chapter 6

SET FREE—SET APART

SET FREE

We all want to lead people into freedom; but before we can lead them there, we need to become free ourselves. In the first chapters of John, we see Jesus going to different places to teach about the nature of God in Him.

> "My teaching is not my own. It comes from the one who sent me" (John 7:16).

Jesus is trying to teach people how to BELIEVE, UNDERSTAND, LEARN and KEEP His teachings. He finally gives the ultimate revelation about His teachings in John 8.

"To the Jews who had believed him, Jesus said,
'If you hold to my teaching, you are really my
disciples. Then you will know the truth, and the
truth will set you free'" (John 8:31, 32).

Jesus was very clear to those who believed Him that to
become free, they had to not only believe in Him, but they still
had to continue to OBEY and remain FAITHFUL to His Word.
Then, they could be called His disciples and His truth would
set them free. Just memorizing His truth won't set us free! Just
listening to His truth won't set us totally free, either. But letting
the truth of God invade our hearts to change our lives will
definitely set us free!

When the Word of God says LOVE, and we don't Love, we
are in bondage. When the Word of God says FORGIVE, and we
can't forgive, we are in bondage. When the Word of God says
DO NOT HAVE ANY OTHER GODS, and we have other gods
in our lives, we are in bondage. When the Word of GOD says
WORSHIP ME WITH JOY AND THANKSGIVING, SING
SPIRITUAL SONGS, BLESS THE NAME OF GOD, and we
show up Sunday morning with APATHY in His presence, we
are in bondage.

"But whoever looks intently into the perfect
law that gives freedom, and continues in it—not
forgetting what they have heard, but doing it—
they will be blessed in what they do" (James 1:25).

Jesus died for us so that we could enjoy freedom! Let this truth set us free from religion, apathy, fear, lack of knowledge, weakness, principalities, powers, the rulers of darkness, sin, doubt, bitterness, addictions or any lie that has covered our eyes for years! He wants us to take a step of faith and let Him in. He wants to make us whole, change our hearts, not only so that we can have an amazing relationship with Him, but also so that we may be free, as He spoke about in the Book of John.

> "So Jesus was saying to those Jews who had believed Him, 'If you continue in My Word, then you are truly disciples of Mine; and you will know the truth, and the truth will make you free.' They answered Him, 'We are Abraham's descendants and have never yet been enslaved to anyone; how is it that You say, 'You will become free?' Jesus answered them, 'Truly, truly, I say to you, everyone who commits sin is the slave of sin. The slave does not remain in the house forever; the son does remain forever. So if the Son makes you free, you will be free indeed'" (John 8:33-36, NASB).

Jesus is talking about people who continue to be in bondage from sin. How can I lead people into freedom if I have not experienced freedom yet for myself? The biggest problem is that it's hard to recognize that we are in bondage.

Here is a great example of this:

"... We are Abraham's descendants and have never

been slaves of anyone. How can you say that we shall be set free?" (John 8:33).

When we look back at the history of Israel, we see that they had been in bondage to many nations; and during that time, they were in bondage to the Romans!

How hard is it for people to recognize their own reality? Most of the time, we don't want to face our own reality, and so we start a battle within ourselves. In this battle for freedom, we are our own worst enemy!

OUR BLIND SIDE

We all have a blind side—things that we cannot notice ourselves. I have met people who could not see what they were doing wrong, and instead of asking for God's direction, they blamed others for their misfortune. What if we came to the conclusion that we didn't know what we were doing and that WE were the problem! What if we came to the conclusion that we are still bitter from a situation that happened to us years ago, and we still can't forgive? What if we came to the realization that what we have been doing for years is a dead religion and not what Jesus intended for us? What if we understood that we needed help because we can't overcome hidden sin and addictions that become normal and familiar over the years? What if we realize that we have relationship problems, and that's the reason why we can't keep friends or be a good leader?

These realizations will only happen when we ask the Holy Spirit to reveal the truth in our lives. Asking the Holy Spirit to show our blind spots is one of the most important prayers we make. We all have blind spots that we cannot see; and that's where we usually get hit by the enemy.

When I was a teenager, one of my friends invited a bunch of us kids to go on an adventure. He was going to borrow his dad's car, without his knowledge or consent, and we would go for a ride. He was learning how to drive, and in his own mind he was ready to drive his dad's car without any supervision or help. We all got inside the car, hoping for the best, as we were not sure if he really knew how to drive or not! He turned the ignition on, fixed the mirrors, wiggled the stick shift and then ... nothing happened. He continued repeating these actions for a long time, but he would not back the car out of the garage.

I started to ask myself if this was a good idea because clearly this kid was not ready to drive! After five minutes of intense preparation, he finally started backing up and suddenly we heard this loud noise, but he didn't stop. He continued driving in reverse until someone screamed, "Stop!" We all jumped out of the car and there it was! A big metal bar sticking out of the wall, which almost sliced the car in half! That metal bar was in our "blind spot."

We need the Holy Spirit to show us the dangers that are hidden in our blind spots. We ask Him, and He will reveal it to us. Has God ever revealed His truth to you during a song or a Word, and you have had a bad response? We are all afraid of knowing the truth and walking in freedom. As worshippers, we believe that our authentic praise and worship lives will declare that we are free from principalities, powers and rulers of darkness and sin.

Our authentic worship is based in humbleness and in a willingness to let go of all strongholds in our lives. It has the power to break every chain. The Lord has placed on us the responsibility to be His vessels, not only through the music we play and sing, but also through our actions. I ask the Lord to show the truth about myself everyday in my worship time. If you make a decision to do the same, be ready to handle what comes from it. Commit to change, and let Jesus guide you in His truth! Let freedom reign!

> **AS WORSHIPPERS, WE BELIEVE THAT OUR AUTHENTIC PRAISE AND WORSHIP LIVES WILL DECLARE THAT WE ARE FREE FROM PRINCIPALITIES, POWERS AND RULERS OF DARKNESS AND SIN.**

"The Spirit of the Lord is on me, because he has anointed me to proclaim good news to the poor. He has sent me to proclaim freedom for the prisoners and recovery of sight for the blind, to set the oppressed free ..." (Luke 4:18).

SET APART

Have you ever thought that the worship of a speech-impaired person could possibly touch the Father's heart more than our praise team or church choir? There's nothing special in our music, if it's not played or sung by people with the right heart.

The singers and musicians in the Divine order of Music were

not just "performers." They were also separated to worship God and influence people with their anointed sound.

That's when worship leaders (musicians and singers) have the opportunity to prove their faithfulness to God. When God sets you apart—He separates your talent, your instrument, your voice and your hands; your whole life belongs to God! Everything about your worship is for the Glory of the Lord. Even more than seeking a carrier in music, God wants you to shine His light.

I know we are not perfect, but as ministers, we should be willing to reach a new standard in our lives if we are called to lead people in worship. Are you willing to give up some of the bad habits that go against God's principles? Are you willing to remain faithful?

As leaders, it is very important that we understand the serious consequences we will face if we have unprepared and unqualified people ministering from the platform. I spoke about our role as priests in the first chapter, and we all know our responsibility in carrying God's presence. The manifestation of His presence is what makes church an awesome place to be, and we don't want to lose that.

My father always said, "God's presence is everywhere. His manifestation is just in a few places." Without the manifestation of God's presence, good music, small groups and great sermons are pointless. God will remove His favor when sin and the lack of a commitment is present, but ignored.

Eli was a man of God, but he failed when he ignored his son's immoral behavior. He forsook the Tabernacle and the presence of God was gone. He honored man and dishonored God. People did what was right in their own eyes. They kept their traditions, bringing their sacrifices, but God's presence wasn't in their midst anymore. Eli experienced the greatest failure of his life, he lost God's Glory in their midst. After his death, his daughter-in-law named her child ICHABOD, which means, "The Glory is Gone."

If we can't fully understand the importance of character in the life of our worship, how can we expect to usher the presence of God into our churches? We need His presence to be manifested, and if His presence is not operating, how can we expect our churches to be agents of transformation?

The day that David was anointed by Samuel, the Scriptures say,

> "... from that day on the Spirit of the LORD came powerfully upon David" (1 Samuel 16:13).

God wants us to SHOW FORTH His Glory in every possible way! Otherwise, there's a big possibility that we'll become the masters of our instrument, instead of being an instrument in the hands of our Master! I frequently ask people, "Why do you want to be a part of the worship team?"

Why do I ask this question? Because I want people to understand that worship isn't primarily about our talent or our love of music. It's about our heart. It's about Whom we love more than anything else.

Our primary concern isn't how great we will sound on Sunday mornings, but the state of our heart. Our music will reflect the relationship we have with God every time we minister to Him.

Talented musicians should be very welcomed in our worship ministries, and I continuously pray to God to keep sending us skillful musicians, but the truth of the matter is, we don't have to be better at our skills, if our hearts are not being purified and set apart. If the desires of our sinful nature are greater than our desire for sanctification, we will find ourselves struggling to offer authentic worship.

When we set our lives apart, character becomes our skeleton. The world applauds talent; as a result, character often comes in second place. God will always choose trustworthiness and character over talent. Trustworthiness and character are in your inner being. In our inner being, we find who we are, which affects everything we do. If the skeleton is not strong enough, the body will break down. That happens when we have plenty of passion, gifts and talents without enough character to hold it all together.

When we show up on Sunday mornings to offer fake worship, we give dominion for the darkness to defeat us. We need to overcome strongholds that are preventing us from releasing the sound of Heaven in our churches. Only a heart in connection with Heaven can release this sound. We need to remind ourselves that without our God, we are only very expensive instruments,

> **... THE TRUTH OF THE MATTER IS, WE DON'T HAVE TO BE BETTER AT OUR SKILLS, IF OUR HEARTS ARE NOT BEING PURIFIED AND SET APART.**

standing on the doorstep of a music store.

David's songs were eternalized and became number one on the music billboard of his time because all his songs came out of a special place—a relationship with God. He wrote songs that exalted the Lord, and He changed the way people worshiped because he set himself apart.

QUESTIONS FOR REFLECTION

1. Can a person be in bondage while going to church? Explain why.

_____

_____

_____

_____

2. How can your blind spots be brought to light?

_____

_____

_____

_____

3. Explain the words "set apart."

_____

_____

_____

_____

Chapter 7

UNDERSTANDING WORSHIP

Our primary goal should be to worship according to God's pattern. And, according to God's pattern, the only acceptable sacrifice is the spiritual sacrifice (sacrifice from the heart). In the Davidic Tabernacle, everyone worshiped the King of kings by expressing their adoration, not because they were obligated to, but because that was the right response to God's presence.

I am part of a group of people who grew up playing and singing music; for many of us, separating music from worship is almost impossible. For this group of people, music can be easily placed in the center of their worship lives.

If we let music become the center of our worship, then we will have a huge problem! We will have a problem because we will limit our sacrifice of praise to our musical abilities only. It's like going back to the tabernacle of Moses where a sacrifice of praise was defined by what they did and not who they were.

We make a big mistake when we allow our worship ministries and congregations to believe that worship is music. We cannot base our worship lives on music, because we will allow worship to be about our musical culture, a particular music generation, our preferences, our tastes and our musical styles. Worship music is always evolving. Worship music was very different when I was a teenager, and it will be very different thirty years from now. Music is ever-changing and unless we have a time machine, we should not base our worship life in music or liturgy. It will always be forever changing with time.

On the other hand, music is much more than artistic expression or entertainment. Music is a tool to use in worshipping our Creator, declare what God has done, what He's doing and what He's going to do.

We need to understand the new seasons in worship music and adapt to it. Worship is about expressing our love to God in everything we do. It's about being an expression of worship—with or without music.

It's about BECOMING WORSHIP and not performing worship, and not being totally dependent on and only wanting to worship with the music that we personally like.

In the New Testament, we find the word *Proskuneo* for

worship, not music. It carries the idea of falling down to kiss God's feet. Worship is an expression of love. When we fall down to kiss the King's feet, there's no pride, and we are totally submitted to Him and His ways, which are always better than ours. We demonstrate God's value in our lives.

> **MUSIC IS A TOOL TO USE IN WORSHIPPING OUR CREATOR, DECLARE WHAT GOD HAS DONE, WHAT HE'S DOING AND WHAT HE'S GOING TO DO.**

Worship starts when we realize Who our King is, and we sacrifice our lives for something of worth. When we understand this principle, our actions become worship, we become worship.

So then, how do we present worship properly? A powerful example in the Book of Romans states,

"Therefore, I urge you, brothers and sisters, in view of God's mercy, to offer your bodies as a living sacrifice, holy and pleasing to God—this is your true and proper worship. Do not conform to the pattern of this world, but be transformed by the renewing of your mind. Then you will be able to test and approve what God's will is—his good, pleasing and perfect will" (Romans 12:1, 2).

Every time we hear the word *sacrifice*, we have a bad picture in our minds because we associate sacrifice with suffering, but that's not what God is saying in these Scriptures. Worship is expressed in obedience to Him. Being obedient to His Word shouldn't be a sacrifice, when we are filled with the Spirit of God.

"If you love me, keep my commands" (John 14:15).

WORSHIP IS OBEDIENCE

How well we are doing, if we brag about our love for Jesus with our songs and instruments, but we can't walk in obedience?

Half obedience is not obedience. For example, the fact that you keep yourself away from pornography doesn't mean you are being obedient if you are sowing discord among the people. Being obedient to God goes beyond fighting and avoiding only the sexual sin. Sin is also operating strongly in our lives when we have bad assumptions, when we judge, when we gossip, turning brothers against brothers, or when our hearts are filled with anger, envy and jealousy.

> **WORSHIP IS EXPRESSED IN OBEDIENCE TO HIM. BEING OBEDIENT TO HIS WORD SHOULDN'T BE A SACRIFICE, WHEN WE ARE FILLED WITH THE SPIRIT OF GOD.**

We can fast for a month, we can spend three hours shouting to God and seeking His face, but if we can't be obedient to His Word, we are not being true worshippers. Obedience is not religion or works. If you feel forced to obey God, but your heart doesn't belong to Him, then it's not worship. Worship is when you chose to serve and obey God out of love and a desire for a close relationship with Him.

Jesus said in the Book of Matthew,

> "Therefore everyone who hears these words of mine and puts them into practice is like a wise man who built his house on the rock" (Matthew 7:24).

Are we being obedient and building our lives, churches and ministries on a Rock?

In the Old Testament, God used the word *obedience* in order to keep His covenant and bless His people.

> "Now if you obey me fully and keep my covenant, then out of all nations you will be my treasured possession" (Exodus 19:5).

> "And this is love: that we walk in obedience to his commands. As you have heard from the beginning, his command is that you walk in love" (2 John 1:6).

Being obedient is God's way of receiving true worship from us. When we obey the Father, we worship the Father.

IN SPIRIT AND TRUTH

The fact that God is looking for those who will worship Him in spirit and truth, proves that these kinds of worshippers are in very short supply.

> "But the hour is coming, and now is, when the true

worshippers will worship the Father in spirit and truth; for the Father is seeking such to worship Him" (John 4:23, NKJV).

But what does it mean to worship God in spirit and in truth? Worshiping God in spirit and truth means to worship Him with the understanding of Who God is and with our whole heart. This kind of worship will reflect His anointing and authority. There's no other way to worship God or to respond to His presence, but in spirit and truth. This principle can't be changed!

> **THE FACT THAT GOD IS LOOKING FOR THOSE WHO WILL WORSHIP HIM IN SPIRIT AND TRUTH, PROVES THAT THESE KINDS OF WORSHIPPERS ARE IN VERY SHORT SUPPLY.**

Worship expressions are a part of our praise and worship, but we should never measure our worship by looking at people's expressions during corporate worship. All expressions we see can be imitated and faked. Real worship is based on the fruit that is coming from their lives. When the church worships in spirit and truth, we see God manifesting Himself in their lives, and their worship expressions are a "real and true" reflection of their genuine and authentic hearts.

Any person who genuinely worships becomes a floodgate when they open their mouths. He or she can open the gate, and bring forth the river of life and the Spirit of the Lord. On the other hand, a person can also bring forth a river of death, the spirit of man, human ego and pride.

We need to flow within—even if we don't like the situations we are facing, or if we don't like the worship leader on Sunday mornings, or the songs they pick. God expects us to be a gate, and we will be blessed every time we open our mouths to become a floodgate of life. The state of our hearts will define what kind of river we are releasing.

Our lifestyle of worship will always help us empty ourselves, so we can be filled by the Spirit of God. Our worship lives are constantly challenged by the battle between our flesh and our spirit. You do have faith, but because you are not consistent in your worship life, you let the flesh rule and become stronger. Then the soul becomes filled with sadness instead of joy, anger instead of love, bitterness instead of forgiveness, and ego instead of humbleness.

When we BECOME WORSHIP, our hearts are soaked with the Spirit of God, and faith rises stronger. David's relationship with God was powerful. His powerful prayers became his authentic worship turned into songs (see Psalm 22:1, and Psalm 23:1-6).

I want to use my wife as an example of authentic worship. My wife is one of the greatest worshippers I know. I became a better worshipper after I married her. Do you think the fact that she has no musical ability makes her less valuable to God? Of course not!

I'll never forget the day that I got home from work and Wanessa was singing in the shower in a very loud voice. I turned the TV on to watch the news, as usual, but her voice was louder than my TV speakers! I asked her to stop singing and she stopped right away. In that moment, God spoke to me clearly. "Why did you cut her off from worshiping Me?" When I heard that, I felt very guilty. Think about it! You don't want to be the person who keeps someone from worshiping God! Immediately, I turned the TV off and I ran to my wife saying, "Honey, don't listen to me! Please, just keep worshiping the Lord! In my mind, she was just singing out of tune, but in the spiritual realm, she was worshiping God in spirit and truth! She was pleasing God, until I suddenly interrupted her!

There are many people out there who can't tell the difference between a minor and a major chord, and they are true worshippers. They might not be called to be in the vocational music ministry, but in God's eyes they have the same value as someone who studied music at Berkeley College.

GOD-CENTERED WORSHIP

We are living in the days where our theology, our doctrine, our beliefs, our vision, our aspirations, and even "our-selves" can become the center of our worship. We think we are worshiping God, but we are worshiping our motives! Today, with all of the information we have about worship, many still cannot understand the subject. The fact that we come together every week does not mean that we are being effective in corporate and personal worship lives.

In ancient times, people would worship the gods and tell them the desires of their hearts, in order to get something in exchange. If I want it to have ten kids, I would worship the god of fertility. If I desired power and money, I would worship the god of money and power! People thought that if they prayed to these false gods, they would obtain what they wanted. Their motives were the center of their worship.

Our corporate and personal worship should emphasize GOD and not ourselves. It should always point to Jesus. That's when worship becomes powerful. When Jesus is not the center, worship becomes meaningless! God inhabits our corporate worship when we praise Him for Who He is.

Many worship the great I Am with the self-centered mentality of seeking their own interests. That's NOT worship! Many have been worshiping the right God, but the wrong way for centuries. They come to the feet of the Great I AM every week with something else placed in the center of their worship.

God-centered worship is not one of the ways of worship. It is actually the ONLY way to worship. Many churches around the globe haven't experienced the benefits and the blessings of a God-centered worship yet. All they know is self-centered worship. Self-centered worship is all about US, ME, MY. It's not about HIM. The main focus of worship is wrong when it becomes our emotions and needs, not God's sovereignty.

God-centered worship will

> MANY HAVE BEEN WORSHIPING THE RIGHT GOD THE WRONG WAY FOR CENTURIES. THEY COME TO THE FEET OF THE GREAT I AM EVERY WEEK WITH SOMETHING ELSE PLACED IN THE CENTER OF THEIR WORSHIP.

exalt God and affirm His abilities. God-centered worship will reveal God's attributes and His character. Out of this worship we get to experience God's Glory and His presence, working actively in our congregations. We will experience unity, people will get saved, marriages will be restored and reconciliations will happen when God become the center of our worship. God-centered worship will allow us to express our adoration to God with no reservations, pouring out to Him what's in our minds, in our hearts and in our souls.

PRAISING

The more intimate the relationship is, the more passion there will be expressed in our worship. Many grew up thinking that it was okay to worship God with their hands in their pocket, not expressing their love and adoration. Their lack of belief and worship knowledge left them lost and blinded for generations. Praise is the expression of worship.

> "Let everything that breathes sing praises to the Lord!" (Psalm 150:6, NLT).

I was in Haiti in May of 2013, with thirteen people on a short-term mission trip. I still remember the praise and worship that took place in this small village in Leogane, Haiti. After three days of hard work, ministering and training the local church, we were finally ready to go back home. We got to the airport, but found out that no flight was leaving the country because of an accident on the runway. No one could give us accurate information as to when or how we would go back home. After three intense hours of frustrated attempts to leave Haiti, we finally realized that the best thing to do, at that moment, was to go back to the village. We went back, but didn't know when we would go home.

Before we left to the airport, we gave all our clothes to the people of the village. All we had in that moment was the clothes we were wearing. People were very worried about our situation because no one knew when we were going to be able to come back to the states. The ladies couldn't communicate with their husbands and children. The whole time I was trying to think of something to say that would bring them back together as a group. Later I realized that no words could do what praise did. We had two options—spend our next days murmuring, or we could praise God!

When the night came, we gathered everyone around and we praised the Lord under the moonlight. There were no instruments and no microphones, just our voices and the rhythms provided by an old empty bucket. We started to praise the Lord and joy filled everyone's heart. At the end of the night, our faces were brighter, and we all felt from the Holy Spirit that we were not done yet in that village. We remained in Haiti two more days, and we were able to evangelize, so many more people were ministered to and we finished everything we had started.

Our praise that night was a declaration that God was faithful, regardless of the situation we found ourselves in! The word praise in Hebrew is *Hallal*. It is the origin of the word, Hallelujah, and is a primitive root that means: to celebrate, to boast, or to make a show.

The first 13 verses of Psalm 148 use the word *Hallal*.

"Praise (*hallal*) the LORD. Praise (*hallal*) the LORD from the heavens; praise Him in the heights above. Praise (*hallal*) Him, all His angels; praise Him, all His heavenly hosts. Praise (*hallal*) Him, sun and moon; praise Him, all you shining stars. Praise (*hallal*) Him, you highest heavens and you waters above the skies. Let them praise (*hallal*) the name of the LORD, for at His command they were created, and He established them forever and ever—He issued a decree that will never pass away. Praise (*hallal*) the LORD from the earth, you great sea creatures and all ocean depths. Lightning and hail, snow and clouds, stormy winds that do His bidding, you mountains and all hills, fruit trees and all cedars, wild animals and all cattle, small creatures and flying birds, kings of the earth and all nations, you princes and all rulers on earth, young men and women, old men and children, let them praise (*hallal*) the name of the LORD, for His name alone is exalted; His splendor is above the earth and the heavens" (Psalm 148:1-13).

We need to keep reminding ourselves that we praise God because He is excellent; His glory is above all and everything. We praise Him because He called us out of the darkness into his marvelous light (see 1 Peter 2:9). We Praise Him for Who He is and what He has done. We praise him because His Attributes and character never change.

I had the opportunity to minister in Los Angeles, California for two weeks with an urban field outreach ministry. We encountered so many young people who had gone to Los Angeles to try to make it with their gifts and talents, but many of them didn't make it. They ended up on the streets, totally devoted to the enemy with all kinds of addictions.

One night, we were ministering on the Walk of Fame, and we found ourselves frustrated after failing several attempts to engage the crowd with our plays. We decided to change our strategy. We began to praise the Lord with upbeat songs about freedom. A few minutes later, we had a big crowd around us.

By the end of the night, we were able to listen to them, pray and share God's love to most of them. We knew that a spiritual battle was taking place in that moment, and we didn't stop singing until we defeated the adversary. Many people were delivered that night by the power of praise.

Praise has the power to break every chain, tear down every stronghold and bring life to a heart in complete darkness. The Bible assures us that God inhabits the praises of His people. This means that if we are not praising God, then He will not inhabit our lives. Sometimes, I see people refusing to express their love to God. There are always excuses to not do so. If you have a congregation that is not praising God, you should really be concerned. The purpose of Sunday mornings is not to put together a little concert so that people can watch us and say how good our "music" is. Worship was never intended to be a spectator sport.

"Praise the LORD. Sing to the LORD a new song, his praise in the assembly of his faithful people. Let Israel rejoice in their Maker; let the people of Zion be glad in their King. Let them praise his name with dancing and make music to him with timbrel and harp. For the LORD takes delight in his people; he crowns the humble with victory. Let his faithful people rejoice in this honor and sing for joy on their beds. May the praise of God be in their mouths and a double-edged sword in their hands, to inflict vengeance on the nations and punishment on the peoples, to bind their kings with fetters, their nobles with shackles of iron, to carry out the sentence written against them—this is the glory of all his faithful people. Praise the LORD" (Psalm 149:1-9).

"Praise be to the God and Father of our Lord Jesus Christ! In his great mercy he has given us new birth into a living hope through the resurrection of Jesus Christ from the dead ..." (1 Peter 1:3).

"But you are a chosen people, a royal priesthood, a holy nation, God's special possession, that you may declare the praises of him who called you out of darkness into his wonderful light" (1 Peter 2:9).

MORE BIBLICAL EVIDENCE:
Philippians 4:8, Psalm 47:1, Ephesians 5:18-20, Psalm 34:1, Psalm 47:6, Romans 15:11, Psalm 7:17, Psalm 71:14, Psalm 95:1, 2, Psalm 107:8, Isaiah 25:1, Revelation 5:12, 13.

QUESTIONS FOR REFLECTION

1. What are the practical examples of worshipping God in Spirit and Truth?

   _____

   _____

   _____

   _____

2. How can disobedience influence your worship life?

   _____

   _____

   _____

   _____

3. What are the things that could be placed at the center of your worship?

   _____

   _____

   _____

   _____

4. Can you describe *praise* with your own words?

_____

_____

_____

_____

5. Can you describe *worship* with your own words?

_____

_____

_____

_____

Chapter 8

WORSHIP IS ALL INCLUSIVE

There are three elements in our lives that need to be engaged in worship:
- Our Knowledge
- Our Heart
- Our Body

OUR KNOWLEDGE

Our relationship with God is based on the understanding of Who God is, what He has done for us and what He expects from us. We need to know the God we worship to be able to worship Him.

I am not saying that God cannot touch a person who doesn't know anything about Him during worship. In fact, God touches people's lives when He is in their midst; but for an individual to become a worshipper, they need to be TRANSFORMED by the Word of God. Otherwise, it just becomes expressed and experienced feelings and not genuine worship. Our worship becomes powerful—not because it's based on feelings alone, but in our conviction and surrender to God's truth in our lives.

OUR HEART

If our hearts are not on fire for God after knowing the truth, there's a high possibility that we just gained head knowledge, which means that our worship has become only an intellectual response to God. The problem with this is if it's only an intellectual response—it's NOT WORSHIP.

The knowledge of Who our God is should transform our hearts and soul (mind, will, and emotions), and ignite our passion in worship. We can have head knowledge and the conviction of Who God is, but if the truth we know is not connected to our hearts, then it's not worship. No matter how much Scripture we know, our heart will only reflect who we are as worshippers when we obey the Scriptures and humble ourselves before God. We must let our heart lead us to experience transformation, and then our feelings toward God will become real.

OUR BODY

Expressing our worship is a biblical command. We can see, know and understand a lot about what a person is feeling by looking at their body language. Our bodies EXPRESS what we KNOW and what we FEEL in worship. Our faces express our passion in our worship. What we KNOW will stir great FEELINGS toward God; and these feelings must be EXPRESSED, not only during corporate worship, but in every action.

Some generations experienced worship, but it was only with their head knowledge. They knew so much about the Bible, and they had a great conviction about the God they were singing about, but they lacked heart. They lacked passion, and they never expressed their convictions and feelings in their worship. The most powerful experiences I have had in worship were when I was expressing my love, reverence and adoration to God. When we retain the expressions we should be revealing, we also retain the pleasure in worship that we were created to experience.

Worship is extremely powerful and effective when we have the knowledge that transforms feelings and our physical expressions of worship by pointing to God.

WORSHIP AND THE IDENTITY OF THE TRINITY

We can't deny that this subject is kind of confusing and paradoxical. No matter how much we study about God, all we will ever be able to see is a shadow of Who He really is. God is so much more than what we understand and believe Him to be. Trying to explain the Trinity is a very ambitious task. So, my job, in the next few pages, is not to explain Who God is, but to give you a basic understanding of the God we serve and worship. After all, worship is real with the basic understanding of Who our God is and what He has done for us.

Because of our limited minds, many have misunderstood the identity of the Trinity; many heresies were born when people tried to explain the Trinity outside of God's revelation. When people misunderstand the identity of the Trinity, they misunderstand the identity of God.

Without a relationship and understanding of the Father, the Son and the Holy Spirit, there is no salvation. Without salvation, there's no worship. We can easily have dead worship when we don't understand the Trinity by faith.

In the past few years, I have seen a new kind of worship leader. They are raising questions like: "Why write so many songs about the cross, Jesus and His sacrifice? Why not write more songs about the Holy Spirit and His power?" Others think we should only talk and preach about Jesus; let's not sing about the Holy Spirit or the creator. This is the mentality of those who don't understand the Trinity. They are always leaning toward one or another.

The Scriptures give us the revelation of an eternal God, Who has revealed Himself as one God, existing in three persons. They are distinguishable, but indivisible in essence. They are coequal in nature, attributes and power.

We can't experience the fullness of God in our lives when we unconsciously see God the Father, God the Son and God the Spirit as three different Gods, or we value one of Them more than another. We can't experience the fullness of God in our worship lives when we separate Jesus' commandments, message and sacrifice from God the Father and God the Holy

Spirit. We can't forget about the Father's acceptance, the Son's sacrifice and the power of the Holy Spirit, operating in glory today.

These are the words of Jesus before ascending to Heaven, "... But you know him, for he lives with you and will be in you. I will not leave you as orphans; I will come to you. Before long, the world will not see me anymore, but you will see me. Because I live, you also will live. On that day you will realize that I am in my Father, and you are in me, and I am in you" (John 14:17-20).

GOD, THE FATHER

The knowledge of the existence of God starts in Genesis. It's not a surprise that Genesis is the most attacked book in the Bible. In Genesis 1:1, the Bible doesn't attempt to prove the existence of God, it simply declares it by saying, "In the beginning God." Faith is the only thing connecting our worship to this eternal God. By faith, we believe in the existence of God; by faith, we worship Him.

We worship a God Who is:
1. Self-existent
2. All knowing, all-powerful and is present everywhere
3. God is our sovereign Creator, Lord and Master
4. Perfect in holiness, righteousness and love
5. God is eternal and faithful

GOD, THE SON

Scripture reveals that Jesus Christ is the eternal Son of God. He always existed with the Father and the Holy Spirit. Because of mankind's disobedience, the relationship between mankind and a Holy God was broken. Jesus took on the form of a man and became our God-man on Earth. In Jesus we find two natures: a Divine nature and the human nature.

Jesus came to Earth to become our hope of becoming acceptable to the Father once again. Jesus came to bring a resolution between sinful man and a holy God. He came on Earth to be the only sacrificial Mediator between God and mankind. He is the Lamb of God, Lord of lords, and the King of kings. God, in Jesus Christ, reveals the plan of salvation. Apart from who Jesus is and what he has done, there's no other way to the Father (see John 14:1-6).

Worship becomes impossible without the knowledge of the atonement and propitiation of God in Jesus Christ. Do you wonder why we have so many songs and lyrics about Jesus, the cross and His sacrifice? Because He is still the doorway to the Trinity, the Kingdom of God, and eternal life. In Jesus, we find the heart of the Father and the power of the Holy Spirit. His message and teachings shape our hearts with a new covenant of love and grace. Eternal life is only available because of Jesus Christ.

GOD, THE HOLY SPIRIT

The Holy Spirit is the third Divine Person of the eternal Godhead. His ministry is to convict and point man to the revelation of Jesus and the Father to the believer. The doctrine of the Holy Spirit is one of the most important doctrines in the Word of God and also the most misinterpreted doctrine in the Bible. The Holy Spirit is not an energy or a force. The Holy Spirit is a person. The Holy Spirit is God.

"Then Peter said, 'Ananias, how is it that Satan has so filled your heart that you have lied to the Holy Spirit and have kept for yourself some of the money you received for the land? Didn't it belong to you before it was sold? And after it was sold, wasn't the money at your disposal? What made you think of doing such a thing? You have not lied just to human beings but to God'" (Acts 5:3, 4).

"And do not grieve the Holy Spirit of God, with whom you were sealed for the day of redemption" (Ephesians 4:30).

Jesus said that if we believed in Him and obeyed His commands, He would send the Holy Spirit, Who would never leave us. Trusting, listening and seeking the Holy Spirit are natural actions, if we are in Christ.

"If you love me, keep my commands. And I will ask the Father, and he will give you another advocate to help you and be with you forever—" (John 14:15, 16).

The Holy Spirit is our Advocate, our Counselor and our Defender. Since The Holy Spirit is operating today in Glory and power, we will spend a little more time on the third person of the Trinity.

UNWRAPPING THE GIFTS OF THE HOLY SPIRIT AND BEARING THE SWEETEST FRUITS

I still remember my Christmas mornings when I was a kid. I couldn't wait to hold my Christmas gift. The anticipation was so intense that I could barely sleep until I finally got my gift. My gift was not supposed to stay under the tree forever, and sooner or later, I would have to unwrap it to find out what was inside that beautiful Christmas wrapping.

Once we come to Christ, the Holy Spirit dwells in us and gives us gifts for His glory. He really wants us to unwrap and use these gifts, just like a child on Christmas morning. Many times, we receive these great gifts from God, and we don't even show any sign of interest in unwrapping them or finding out what they are.

WHEN WE LIVE AN AUTHENTIC WORSHIP LIFE WITH THE HOLY SPIRIT, WE SEE THE GIFTS AND THE FRUIT DISPLAYED EQUALLY IN OUR LIVES. IF THAT IS NOT THE CASE, WE MAY NOT EXPERIENCE THE HOLY SPIRIT IN OUR LIVES, BUT OUR OWN SPIRIT.

When you discover these gifts, you will realize the same power that raised Christ from the dead is available for the Church today and not just for the clergy. We don't need to call on our pastor to pray for our sick child! We can pray, and he or she can be healed. We can and should preach, evangelize, give words of wisdom, and even cast out demons if need be. Many times, we don't do it because we are too busy with what we call our "real job." After all, we have people that get paid to do that! That's a wrong mentality. Remember, we are all ministers!

With these great gifts, comes a great responsibility! We can get really excited about our gifts without the knowledge, preparation or wisdom for their proper scriptural exercise. We can also get carried away by our own personalities, emotions and personal opinions. When we let our flesh rule, people begin to wonder if everything they hear or see is entirely from God, or if any of it is from God at all.

When we live an authentic worship life with the Holy Spirit, we see the gifts and the fruit displayed equally in our lives. If that is not the case, we may not experience the Holy Spirit in our lives, but our own spirit. Producing the fruit of the Spirit and exercising the gifts are vital to our walk with Christ.

Many times, we come to Christ, receive the Holy Spirit, but then don't allow the Him to show His fruit in our daily lives.

"But the fruit of the spirit is love, joy, peace, patience, kindness, goodness, faithfulness, gentleness and self-control ..." (Galatians 5:22, 23, ESV).

It's very easy to display God's fruit during our worship services when the lights are down and the keyboard player is playing the most beautiful worship chords. But how will we react

113

on Monday morning when things like conflict, disappointments, temptations, crisis and disagreements happen? If we are living by the Spirit of God, He will comfort us and lead us into the way we should go. He is the Spirit of Truth. This will help us take control of our thoughts, feelings and actions.

"You, my brothers and sisters, were called to be free. But do not use your freedom to indulge the flesh; rather, serve one another humbly in love. For the entire law is fulfilled in keeping this one command: 'Love your neighbor as yourself.' If you bite and devour each other, watch out or you will be destroyed by each other. So I say, walk by the Spirit, and you will not gratify the desires of the flesh. For the flesh desires what is contrary to the Spirit, and the Spirit what is contrary to the flesh. They are in conflict with each other, so that you are not to do whatever you want. But if the Spirit leads you, you are not under the law. The acts of the flesh are obvious: sexual immorality, impurity and debauchery; idolatry and witchcraft; hatred, discord, jealousy, fits of rage, selfish ambition, dissensions, factions and envy; drunkenness, orgies, and the like. I warn you, as I did before, that those who live like this will not inherit the kingdom of God. But the fruit of the Spirit is love, joy, peace, forbearance, kindness, goodness, faithfulness, gentleness and self-control. Against such things there is no law. Those who belong to Christ Jesus have crucified the flesh with its passions and desires. Since we live by the Spirit, let us keep in step with the Spirit. Let us not become conceited, provoking and envying each other" (Galatians 5:13-26).

Bearing the fruit of the Spirit in our lives will help us face any situation, a proposal or any temptation that could bring disastrous consequences.

"By their fruit you will recognize them. Do people pick grapes from thornbushes, or figs from thistles?" (Matthew 7:16).

"To the angel of the church in Sardis write: These are the words of him who holds the seven spirits of God and the seven stars. I know your deeds; you have a reputation of being alive, but you are dead. Wake up! Strengthen what remains and is about to die, for I have found your deeds unfinished in the sight of my God. Remember, therefore, what you have received and heard; hold it fast, and repent. But if you do not wake up, I will come like a thief, and you will not know at what time I will come to you" (Revelation 3:1-3).

If we want to function the way God designed us to function,

we should definitely grow in our intimacy with the Holy Spirit to have the gifts and the fruit manifested in our worship.

Jesus helped us understand this matter when He said that the Spirit would not testify of Himself, but of Christ.

"When the Advocate comes, whom I will send to you from the Father—the Spirit of truth who goes out from the Father—he will testify about me" (John 15:26).

The scriptural exercise of the gifts and the bearing of the fruit will always point to Jesus Christ and His glory. That's when we will experience unity, edification and the real move of God.

There are times when we find ourselves in a desperate quest to display God's gifts, powers, wonders and miracles, and we forget Who He is and what He has already done in our lives. Our churches can experience God's glory in a powerful way when we entirely surrender to the power of the Holy Spirit. Out of this basic foundation in worship, we will be able to cultivate a relationship with the Holy Spirit and experience everything He has to offer.

ENTIRELY SURRENDERED TO THE POWER OF THE HOLY SPIRIT

Throughout the years, I've seen many people emphasizing one thing and neglecting others. Usually we emphasize something that expresses what WE value the most. As a musician, for example, I could easily emphasize the musical portion of our service and neglect other very important biblical aspects of it. Some people emphasize the prophetic and neglect the power in the Word of God. Others emphasize the Word of God, but neglect the biblical promises of power. Some emphasize love and neglect purity. Others emphasize holiness and neglect the grace of God.

We are living in dark and difficult days, where more than ever, the Church needs to be fully led by the Holy Spirit. It is not an either/or proposition, but it is a both/and situation. If we are to successfully stand before the challenges of our time in love and power, we must have both, the fruit and the gifts of the Holy Spirit. We cannot embrace one and neglect the other.

We must have faith, speak words of wisdom and knowledge, but we also must be patient and kind. We must pray for healing and prophecy, but we also must have character. We must seek His power, but we also must love, forgive and worship in purity. We must have boldness to speak in the authority of God, but we must also walk in humbleness and self-control.

We must entirely embrace the Holy Spirit of God if we want to see the Holy Spirit fully active in our lives today. This subject has been on my mind for years as I witness many people emphasizing only what they value the most in the Spirit of God and also in their walk with Christ.

Is it possible that this is the reason that the Church in the world is so powerless? Somewhere in our journey, we probably began emphasizing one thing and neglecting another.

I believe that God is raising a generation who will not only sing worship songs with passion, but He is raising worshippers who will consecrate and surrender themselves to the power of the Holy Spirit!

QUESTIONS FOR REFLECTION

1. How can you fully engage in Worship?

_____

_____

_____

_____

2. Explain with your own words the phrase, *"Without a relationship and understanding of the Father, the Son and the Holy Spirit, there is no salvation. Without salvation, there's no worship."*

_____

_____

_____

_____

3. Explain how you can fully function in the Spirit. (Gifts and Fruit of the Spirit of God).

_____

_____

_____

_____

Chapter 9

CORPORATE WORSHIP AND MUSIC

"... be filled with the Spirit, speaking to one another with psalms, hymns, and songs from the Spirit. Sing and make music from your heart to the Lord, always giving thanks to God the Father for everything, in the name of our Lord Jesus Christ" (Ephesians 5:18-20).

Many grew up thinking that the purpose of the music in corporate worship was to prepare our hearts for the sermon, but that is not what worship is really all about. Many look at worship as the appetizer, something that would prepare our empty stomachs for the main course. Others look at corporate worship as a way of reinforcing the pastor's message. This mentality neglects the very purpose of corporate worship. Worship God! We don't worship to receive the Word of God better. We receive the Word of God to worship better.

Music was one of the three fundamental professions in establishing the human society. Lamech, Cain's descendent had three sons: Jabal, Jubal and Tubal Cain. Jabal was a herdsman and the father of agriculture. Jubal was a musician and the father of music and the arts. Tubal was the father of industry. Every occupation at that time was generally classified under these three categories, and God chose music to be one of the most powerful expressions of worship in the life of mankind.

Since the beginning of time, we have had a strong and unique association with music and singing in our worship experience. Music was created by God—for God. Before David established God's new order of music in the Tabernacle, music was already a part of the life of the Hebrew people. Music is mentioned in the Old Testament several times (see Exodus 15:2, 20, 21 and Judges 5:3).

God showed His people His plans for music and corporate worship when David established a new order of worship in Jerusalem. They worshiped God with music and a spiritual sacrifice of praise in the Tabernacle. Not coincidently, the people of Israel lived their highest spiritual years under this new order.

This generation sees music as merely cool rhythms and catchy lyrics, but music is so much more than that! We, as worshippers, should have the discernment to know what kind of influence we should allow in our lives.

When we study the Divine Order of Music in the Tabernacle of David, we see that their music and worship was doing more than just affecting people emotionally. Music was actually changing their nation. It was more than just a performance. God spoke through their anointed music to their hearts! Being emotionally affected by music and being touched by God through the power of a heavenly sound isn't the same thing at all.

We want God to do something through our music that can't be explained by music therapeutics. We want the Spirit of the Lord to empower our music. That's when our music and corporate worship becomes an expression of worship that will not only bring the Glory of God, but also bless the people. In the western world we are all about the individualistic ways of doing things. The Hebrew text and culture is always about collective unity and community. That's why their worship and music was blessing God, changing the nation and blessing the people.

> WE DON'T WORSHIP TO RECEIVE THE WORD OF GOD BETTER. WE RECEIVE THE WORD OF GOD TO WORSHIP BETTER.

In the New Testament, we see the Early Church inheriting the joy of music that was established in the Old Testament, even after the destruction of the first temple and their time of captivity in Babylonia. The believers kept using the psalms as a reference in worship in their new era—an era of persecution— where their worship had to be done in hidden places. It was no longer only confined to the temple or synagogues, but in every gathering of believers. They became the Temple, and their worship reflected the joy of the Lord, even in the midst of oppression (see Ephesians 5:19, Colossians 3:16 and Acts 16:25).

In AD 391, Constantine made his best political move by legalizing Christianity. Although, at first, it sounded like a great idea, history proved later that the results were not positive. The Christian church that Constantine promoted was a mixture of true Christianity and Roman paganism. The church went from being primitive to a position of leadership, power and influence, and in just one hundred years, they had built more than five hundred cathedrals.

> **BEING EMOTIONALLY AFFECTED BY MUSIC AND BEING TOUCHED BY GOD THROUGH THE POWER OF A HEAVENLY SOUND ISN'T THE SAME THING AT ALL.**

An empire was built, but it was far from the true message of Jesus Christ. With this unification, the church lost their interest in being ministers, and the identity of true worship was lost, as well. Joy and expression of praise was no longer in the midst of the people, and the clergy dominated every aspect of their liturgical and musical worship life.

Ninety-five percent of the people didn't have access to the truth or any kind of education. The clergy named themselves the highest priests to represent the people with God; and people's corporate worship became totally controlled by man.

Music and expressions of worship remained alive and

strong during the worst years of martyring and persecuting the Christians, but it could not survive when the Roman Empire granted their fake "freedom." Worship became passionless, empty, and was totally ruled by dogmas and pagan traditions. The people's music expressions were in bondage again, just like during the four hundred years of slavery in Egypt.

In the 1500s with Luther leading the reformation period, the people began to experience a new revival in worship again. The people began to have access to the Scriptures, where the Word of God was transforming their minds again. With this new joy in their lives, the desire to express their adoration grew stronger once again. Luther himself said that music was one of the strongest gifts God gave to humanity, and everyone should learn music before being ordained as spiritual leaders.

The many years of worship drought in the Church, caused significant damage, and today, we find ourselves fighting to bring back God's original idea for corporate worship and music. It's time for our generation to claim back the identity of our corporate worship! It's time revive the Church—make it alive again. It's time to experience today what once was. It's time to experience the power of one voice.

"The thief comes only to steal and kill and destroy;
I have come that they may have life, and have it to
the full" (John 10:10).

THE POWER OF ONE VOICE

What would happen if the God's Church realized that exalting

God's name with one voice would produce a new identity in our corporate worship with endless fruit, making our services function the way they are intended to function? Singing in unity with a new mindset, a new perspective and a new motivation will bring Heaven to Earth and make the Church come alive.

When we look at the Divine Order of Music under David, we find a beautiful choir of thousands who are singing to the Lord in one voice. Every person was part of the worship. Singing wasn't only for "singers," or for the clergy. Everyone sang because the Scriptures commanded everyone to do so.

David had all three parts of the corporate worship functioning: He had the leaders (Elders), the musicians and the people worshiping in one accord. If we want to experience a powerful corporate worship, we need to understand that our gathering should always have all three parts of the Church engaged in worship:

- Leadership (pastors, worship leader, elders)
- Musicians (praise band, praise choir, orchestra)
- Congregation (children, young and old)

This is the scriptural way of worship—all three parts joining in our worship gatherings. We should view our congregations as part of our worship team. It is very sad when only two thirds or even one of these three parts is worshiping. Every person should worship God with their praise expressions—bowing down, clapping hands, shouting, lifting their hands, singing and dancing. If we don't have these three parts engaging in worship, something needs to be done.

Today, we can identify three sectors of worshippers in the body of Christ that restrain the Church to worship with one voice:

1. The FIRST SECTOR values traditions and rituals more than God. They fight to keep the dogmas created by personal opinions on what we should look like and what worship should look like. Their agenda is more important than God's agenda. What they know is what they do, and God cannot do anything beyond what they know. They live in the past, and anything new is not very well accepted by them.

2. The SECOND SECTOR is composed of emotionally-driven people, rather than being biblically-truth driven. They measure their love for God according to how high they raise their hands or how loud they can shout during worship. They are free from all church traditions and their worship is passionate. They can sing the same song for hours as long as they "feel good" about singing it.

3. The THIRD SECTOR is the segment of people who actually understand worship. They seek to grow in the Word of God to be transformed, and not just for intellectual information. They love the Lord with all their mind, soul and strength and have a healthy relationship with God and others. They know Who their God is and what He has done for them. That's why their worship lives are a passionate and powerful

expression of love in response to God's presence. They have a missional vision, and they always put God above any ritual, tradition, musical preference or personal opinion.

At one time, my office was inside a worship building. During the week, the place we called our "worship center" was empty and lifeless. If we decided to sell the building, the place that we called "church" could have become a movie theater or a candy factory. There's nothing sacred or special about a building, until it is filled with God's people. That's when it becomes a Holy place and the real church takes place. The empty, cold and dark sanctuary becomes vibrant and alive—becoming a place to connect with God. What is the point of coming to church if we don't connect with God in worship?

The Bible explains that we are the Temple of the Holy Spirit, and Jesus is OUR Temple! To be THE CHURCH, we don't need a building to worship God, but when we gather in His Name, the Holy Spirit in us ignites a passionate worship that we can intensely feel, and most importantly, a worship that will always point to God. That's the kind of praise and worship atmosphere that He inhabits and ministers to us through.

We all know that corporate worship will never replace the importance of private worship. However, we shouldn't neglect the importance of corporate worship, either. The early Christians are almost always seen worshiping, evangelizing, praying and singing together, and that's how their music empowered them to grow spiritually and in numbers.

In the Early Church, Messianic believers found themselves often oppressed, but they also found their way to get beyond their abysmal circumstances in their gatherings. They wrote important music like, "The Odes of Solomon," which were the first hymnals composed by anonymous Messianic believers under very difficult circumstances. They had inspirational worship where they used their expressions of worship passionately. They worshiped with raised hands in gratitude, remembering Jesus' sacrifice.

As in the Old Testament, the overwhelming focus is on corporate worship, not on isolated individuals of God. Corporate worship is crucial to God's purpose for His people. The spiritual life of Israel was accompanied by a commitment to authentic corporate worship. There were no solos, or performance, but the sound of thousands of singers who were all singing with one voice. When the Church comes into agreement with that, we will see what God is able to do! When we express our love and worship corporately, God demonstrates His presence in a unique way.

THERE'S NOTHING SACRED OR SPECIAL ABOUT A BUILDING, UNTIL IT IS FILLED WITH GOD'S PEOPLE.

"Ascribe to the LORD the glory due His name; bring an offering and come before Him. Worship the LORD in the splendor of His holiness" (1 Chronicles 16:29).

Our responsibility as worshippers is to claim back God-centered, corporate worship and the expressions of our hearts in our corporate worship. Worship is not about music, personalities or our own preferences. It is about pleasing God—not mankind. If you touch God, He will touch you back. We were not called to impress, but to EXPRESS!

"May the God who gives endurance and encouragement give you the same attitude of mind toward each other that Christ Jesus had, so that with one mind and one voice you may glorify the God and Father of our Lord Jesus Christ" (Romans 15:5, 6).

Worship goes beyond us. The Church has made worship about musical styles and making music more important than the One we worship. If we want the Church to worship in unity, we need to relocate our hearts to Jesus and not our preferences.

After many years of dead religion and empty rituals, David established a new order of worship. He brought God's presence back, and along with His presence came music, dancing, clapping and shouts of joy! David built a brand new Tabernacle on Mount Zion where EVERYONE had access to God's presence. This Tabernacle was a reflection of God's will for His people through Jesus.

The Tabernacle was a remarkable foreshadowing of Christ's ministry as our High Priest and King. This Tabernacle was clearly a model of the New Testament Church. David's Tabernacle was a giant, Holy of Holies, where His presence was available to everyone and anyone who was seeking Him.

This new Tabernacle was not a renouncement of God's first Tabernacle, the Tabernacle of Moses, but it was a Divine enhancement. David gave the people of God a fresh understanding of praise that reflected the true heart of worship before the Lord. His prayers became songs, and this new worship order changed a nation.

For thirty-three years, David established a twenty-four hour, around-the-clock worship on Mount Zion where worship was expressed in unity and agreement.

God's Church will only experience His tangible presence when we join together in one accord. Our level of worship should never depend on how much we like the music style or the songs. The great outpouring of new worship songs in the past few years has been phenomenal. We now have thousands of songs to choose from. We should try to choose songs that have great potential to work in our local church, but even with all the effort to choose the right songs, we shouldn't expect the whole church to like every song that we bring. We should, however, EXPECT them to worship God!

THE AUTHORITY OF THE SCRIPTURES

Many believe that theology and biblical teachings are the occupations of pastors, teachers, evangelists and missionaries, while singing songs is the occupation of the worship leaders. Because of that, we have many handicapped worship ministries and churches that are limping in the understanding of the scriptural-based worship. Singing, teaching and declaring the

Word of God will wake up people to a deeper relationship with God because their hearts will be passionately filled with the truth of God.

In David's Tabernacle the musicians and singers were not merely using their musical talent. They had to go through seven years of intense training in the word—along with fifteen years of training that was required for those who were called for leadership. There was a price to be paid, if you were willing to be part of the greatest worship team on the whole Earth.

Within the authority of Scripture, lay all the truth of God. Jesus said that when the Word of God is sowed into our hearts, the enemy will come right a way to steal it. Having a right response to God's Word will keep the enemy from stealing this seed from us. Knowing the Scriptures alone won't make you a Worshipper, but the right response will. We become aligned with the Scriptures when we obey His Words, believing in the truth and power of His Word.

When we neglect the Word of God, the Church becomes scripturally illiterate. If at the end of our worship service, all we did was distract people from the Word of God, something needs to be done before it's too late.

As a worship leader, I want people to leave church with something more than a few goose bumps. I want them to grow as believers in Christ! There's nothing wrong with spontaneity in worship and impact phrases of knowledge, but we are living in times where we see the Word of God under attack very clearly. There are those who can sing passionately for hours, but are totally disconnected from the Scriptures; and that's the reason why we have so many people who are inconsistent and weak in our Churches. They come for the roller coaster of emotions, but when the service is over, they go back to the same place of uncertainty and inconsistency in their faith.

People are not being challenged by the Word; therefore, people are not growing or being changed by it. The Bible says in Exodus 16:4 that the Word of God is our "Daily Bread." There are Christians that are dying spiritually because they are not receiving any nutrients from our "Daily Bread."

Our services, songs and personal lives should be filled with God's Word! From "the Word," we should be enabled by the presence of the Spirit of God. Everything we say, everything we sing and minister to the Church should have the truth of the Scriptures, even when we are being moved in the prophetic. God can continually give us new revelations anytime, but these prophetic revelations will never contradict or replace the power of Scripture. We all need to guard our hearts constantly so that we are not carried away by our emotions, saying and doing things that are contrary to the Word of God.

> ... WE SHOULDN'T EXPECT THE WHOLE CHURCH TO LIKE EVERY SONG THAT WE BRING. WE SHOULD, HOWEVER, EXPECT THEM TO WORSHIP GOD!

"For the Word of God is alive and active. Sharper than any double-edged sword, it penetrates even to dividing soul and spirit, joints and marrow; it judges the thoughts and attitudes of the heart" (Hebrews 4:12).

QUESTIONS FOR REFLECTION

1. Explain the importance of music as one of our worship and praise expressions.

_____

_____

_____

_____

2. What did corporate worship look like in the Tabernacle of David, and how can you establish the same kind of corporate worship in your own life?

_____

_____

_____

_____

3. How can you help promote unity in corporate worship?

_____

_____

_____

_____

CONCLUSION

No matter where we are on our worship journey, the faster we grow in our identity, the faster we will become the person God has created us to be. The faster we become the person God has created us to be, the faster we will find out what God's purpose for our lives is.

We should not settle for a worship culture that measures our success as worshippers by our marketing, promotion or mankind's recognition. We should not settle for a worship culture that is motivated by selfish desires. We should not settle for a worship culture that is religiously passionless and apathetic.

As we approach the end of this book, my question is this: Are we convinced that God actually enjoys and validates our worship lives?

My prayer is that everyone should come to answer "YES"

after reading this book. Let's believe, receive and BECOME WORSHIP!

> "But the LORD said to Samuel, 'Do not consider his appearance or his height, for I have rejected him. The LORD does not look at the things people look at. People look at the outward appearance, but the LORD looks at the heart'" (1 Samuel 16:7).

QUICK SCRIPTURE REFERENCES

"Therefore, I urge you, brothers and sisters, in view of God's mercy, to offer your bodies as a living sacrifice, holy and pleasing to God—this is your true and proper worship. Do not conform to the pattern of this world, but be transformed by the renewing of your mind. Then you will be able to test and approve what God's will is—his good, pleasing and perfect will" (Romans 12:1, 2).

"See what kind of love the Father has given to us that we should be called children of God; and so we are. The reason why the world does not know us is that it did not know him" (1 John 3:1).

"The LORD your God is in your midst, a mighty one who will save; he will rejoice over you with gladness; he will quiet you by his love; he will exult over you with loud singing" (Zephaniah 3:17, ESV).

"I will give you a new heart and put a new spirit in you; I will remove from you your heart of stone and give you a heart of flesh" (Ezekiel 36:26).

"Therefore, if anyone is in Christ, the new creation has come: The old has gone, the new is here!" (2 Corinthians 5:17).

"... Speak to us yourself and we will listen. But do not have God speak to us or we will die" (Exodus 20:19).

"But you are a chosen people, a royal priesthood, a holy nation, God's special possession, that you may declare the praises of Him who called you out of darkness into His wonderful light" (1 Peter 2:9).

"... If your Presence does not go with us, do not send us up from here" (Exodus 33:15).

"Paul, a servant of Christ Jesus, called to be an apostle and set apart for the gospel of God—" (Romans 1:1).

"They came to Capernaum. When he was in the house, he asked them, 'What were you arguing about on the road?' But they kept quiet because on the way they had argued about who was the greatest. Sitting down, Jesus called the Twelve and said, 'Anyone who wants to be first must be the very last, and the servant of all'" (Mark 9:33-35).

"Instead, whoever wants to become great among you must be your servant, and whoever wants to be first must be your slave— just as the Son of Man did not come to be served, but to serve, and to give his life as a ransom for many" (Matthew 20:26-28).

"In your relationships with one another, have the same mindset as Christ Jesus: Who, being in very nature God, did not consider equality with God something to be used to his own advantage; rather, he made himself nothing by taking the very nature of a servant, being made in human likeness. And being found in appearance as a man, he humbled himself by becoming obedient to death—even death on a cross!" (Philippians 2:5-8).

"Not that we are competent in ourselves to claim anything for ourselves, but our competence comes from God. He has made us competent as ministers of a new covenant—not of the letter but of the Spirit; for the letter kills, but the Spirit gives life" (2 Corinthians 3:5, 6).

"So Christ himself gave the apostles, the prophets, the evangelists, the pastors and teachers, to equip his people for works of service, so that the body of Christ may be built up until we all reach unity in the faith and in the knowledge of the Son of God and become mature, attaining to the whole measure of the fullness of Christ. Then we will no longer be infants, tossed back and forth by the waves, and blown here and there by every wind of teaching and by the cunning and craftiness of people in their deceitful scheming. Instead, speaking the truth in love, we will grow to become in every respect the mature body of him who is the head, that is, Christ. From him the whole body, joined and held together by every supporting ligament, grows and builds itself up in love, as each part does its work." (Ephesians 4:11-16).

"The Spirit of the LORD is upon me, for He has anointed me to bring Good News to the poor. He has sent me to proclaim that captives will be released, that the blind will see, that the oppressed will be set free ..." (Luke 4:18, NLT).

"For the Kingdom of God is not a matter of eating and drinking, but of righteousness, peace and joy in the Holy Spirit, because anyone who serves Christ in this way is pleasing to God and receives human approval" (Romans 14:17, 18).

"A psalm of praise. Of David. 'I will exalt You, my God the King; I will praise Your name forever and ever. Every day I will praise You and extol Your name forever and ever. Great is the LORD and most worthy of praise; His greatness no one can fathom. One generation commends Your works to another; they tell of Your mighty acts. They speak of the glorious splendor of Your majesty—and I will meditate on Your wonderful works. They tell of the power of Your awesome works and I will proclaim Your great deeds. They celebrate Your abundant goodness and joyfully sing of Your righteousness. The LORD is gracious and compassionate; slow to anger and rich in love. The LORD is good to all; he has compassion on all he has made. All Your works praise You, LORD; Your faithful people extol You. They tell of the glory of Your kingdom and speak of Your might, so that all people may know of Your mighty acts and the glorious splendor of Your kingdom. Your kingdom is an everlasting kingdom, and Your dominion endures through all generations. The LORD is trustworthy in all He promises and faithful in all he does. The LORD upholds all who fall and lifts up all who are bowed down. The eyes of all look to you, and you give them their food at the proper time. You open your hand and satisfy the desires of every living thing. The LORD is righteous in all His ways and faithful in all He does. The Lord is near to all who call on Him, to all who call on Him in truth. He fulfills the desires of those who fear Him; He hears their cry and saves them. The LORD watches over all who love Him, but all the wicked He will destroy. My mouth will speak in praise of the LORD. Let every creature praise His holy name forever and ever'" (Psalm 145:1-21).

"'Teacher, which is the greatest commandment in the Law?' Jesus replied: 'Love the Lord your God with all your heart and with all your soul and with all your mind.' This is the first and greatest commandment. And the second is like it: 'Love your neighbor as yourself.' All the Law and the Prophets hang on these two commandments" (Matthew 22:36-40).

"If I speak in the tongues of men or of angels, but do not have love, I am only a resounding gong or a clanging cymbal. If I have the gift of prophecy and can fathom all mysteries and all knowledge, and if I have a faith that can move mountains, but do not have love, I am nothing. If I give all I possess to the poor and give over my body to hardship that I may boast, but do not have love, I gain nothing" (1 Corinthians 13:1-3).

"Dear friends, let us love one another, for love comes from

God. Everyone who loves has been born of God and knows God. Whoever does not love does not know God, because God is love. This is how God showed his love among us: He sent his one and only Son into the world that we might live through him. This is love: not that we loved God, but that he loved us and sent his Son as an atoning sacrifice for our sins. Dear friends, since God so loved us, we also ought to love one another. No one has ever seen God; but if we love one another, God lives in us and his love is made complete in us. This is how we know that we live in him and he in us: He has given us of his Spirit. And we have seen and testify that the Father has sent his Son to be the Savior of the world. If anyone acknowledges that Jesus is the Son of God, God lives in them and they in God. And so we know and rely on the love God has for us. God is love. Whoever lives in love lives in God, and God in them. This is how love is made complete among us so that we will have confidence on the Day of Judgment: In this world we are like Jesus. There is no fear in love. But perfect love drives out fear, because fear has to do with punishment. The one who fears is not made perfect in love. We love because he first loved us. Whoever claims to love God yet hates a brother or sister is a liar. For whoever does not love their brother and sister, whom they have seen, cannot love God, whom they have not seen" (1 John 4:7-20).

"If I could speak all the languages of earth and of angels, but didn't love others, I would only be a noisy gong or a clanging cymbal. If I had the gift of prophecy, and if I understood all of God's secret plans and possessed all knowledge, and if I had such faith that I could move mountains, but didn't love others, I would be nothing" (1 Corinthians 13:1, 2, NLT).

"Above all else, guard your heart, for everything you do flows from it" (Proverbs 4:23).

"I will give them an undivided heart and put a new spirit in them; I will remove from them their heart of stone and give them a heart of flesh" (Ezekiel 11:19).

"... I will ascend to the heavens; I will raise my throne above the stars of God; I will sit enthroned on the mount of assembly, on the utmost heights of Mount Zaphon. I will ascend above the tops of the clouds; I will make myself like the Most High" (Isaiah 14:13, 14).

"Then Jesus was led by the Spirit into the wilderness to be tempted by the devil. After fasting forty days and forty nights, he was hungry. The tempter came to him and said, 'If you are the Son of God, tell these stones to become bread.' Jesus answered, 'It is written: 'Man shall not live on bread alone, but on every word that comes from the mouth of God.' Then the devil took him to the holy city and had him stand on the highest point of the temple. 'If you are the Son of God,' he said, 'throw yourself down.' For it is written: 'He will command his angels concerning you, and they will lift you up in their hands, so that you will not strike your foot against a stone.' Jesus answered him, 'It is also written: 'Do not put the Lord your God to the test.' Again, the devil took him to a very high mountain and showed him all the kingdoms of the world and their splendor. 'All this I will give you,' he said, 'if you will bow down and worship me.' Jesus said to him, 'Away from me, Satan!' For it is written: 'Worship the Lord your God, and serve him only.' Then the devil left him, and angels came and attended him" (Matthew 4:1-11).

"You shall worship the Lord your God and Him only shall you serve" (Matthew 4:10, ESV).

"He who has clean hands and a pure heart, who does not lift up his soul what is false and does not swear deceitfully" (Psalm 24:4, ESV).

"The fear of the LORD is the beginning of wisdom, and knowledge of the Holy One is understanding" (Proverbs 9:10).

"... let us draw near to God with a sincere heart and with the full assurance that faith brings, having our hearts sprinkled to cleanse us from a guilty conscience and having our bodies washed with pure water" (Hebrews 10:22).

"In the first month of the first year of his reign, he opened the doors of the temple of the LORD and repaired them. He brought in the priests and the Levites, assembled them in the square on the east side and said: 'Listen to me, Levites! Consecrate yourselves now and consecrate the temple of the LORD, the God of your ancestors. Remove all defilement from the sanctuary. Our

142

parents were unfaithful; they did evil in the eyes of the LORD our God and forsook him. They turned their faces away from the LORD'S dwelling place and turned their backs on him. They also shut the doors of the portico and put out the lamps. They did not burn incense or present any burnt offerings at the sanctuary to the God of Israel. Therefore, the anger of the LORD has fallen on Judah and Jerusalem; he has made them an object of dread and horror and scorn, as you can see with your own eyes. This is why our fathers have fallen by the sword and why our sons and daughters and our wives are in captivity. Now I intend to make a covenant with the LORD, the God of Israel, so that his fierce anger will turn away from us. My sons, do not be negligent now, for the LORD has chosen you to stand before him and serve him, to minister before him and to burn incense'" (2 Chronicles 29:3-11).

"The whole assembly bowed in worship, while the musicians played and the trumpets sounded. All this continued until the sacrifice of the burnt offering was completed. When the offerings were finished, the king and everyone present with him knelt down and worshiped. King Hezekiah and his officials ordered the Levites to praise the LORD with the words of David and of Asaph the seer. So they sang praises with gladness and bowed down and worshiped" (2 Chronicles 29:28-30).

"Hezekiah and all the people rejoiced at what God had brought about for his people, because it was done so quickly" (2 Chronicles 29:36).

"Saul has slain his thousands, and David his tens of thousands" (1 Samuel 18:7).

"For those who exalt themselves will be humbled, and those who humble themselves will be exalted" (Matthew 23:12).

"A heart at peace gives life to the body, but envy rots the bones" (Proverbs 14:30).

"It is true that some preach Christ out of envy and rivalry, but others out of goodwill" (Philippians 1:15).

"My teaching is not my own. It comes from the one who sent me" (John 7:16).

"To the Jews who had believed him, Jesus said, 'If you hold to my teaching, you are really my disciples. Then you will know the truth, and the truth will set you free'" (John 8:31, 32).

"But whoever looks intently into the perfect law that gives freedom, and continues in it—not forgetting what they have heard, but doing it—they will be blessed in what they do" (James 1:25).

"... We are Abraham's descendants and have never been slaves of anyone. How can you say that we shall be set free?" (John 8:33).

"The Spirit of the Lord is on me, because he has anointed me to proclaim good news to the poor. He has sent me to proclaim freedom for the prisoners and recovery of sight for the blind, to set the oppressed free ..." (Luke 4:18).

"If you love me, keep my commands" (John 14:15).

"Therefore everyone who hears these words of mine and puts them into practice is like a wise man who built his house on the rock" (Matthew 7:24).

"Now if you obey me fully and keep my covenant, then out of all nations you will be my treasured possession" (Exodus 19:5).

"But the hour is coming, and now is, when the true worshippers will worship the Father in spirit and truth; for the Father is seeking such to worship Him" (John 4:23, NKJV).

"Praise the LORD. Sing to the LORD a new song, his praise in the assembly of his faithful people. Let Israel rejoice in their Maker; let the people of Zion be glad in their King. Let them praise his name with dancing and make music to him with timbrel and harp. For the LORD takes delight in his people; he crowns the humble with victory. Let his faithful people rejoice in this honor and sing for joy on their beds. May the praise of God be in their mouths and a double-edged sword in their hands, to inflict vengeance on the nations and punishment on the peoples, to bind their kings with fetters, their nobles with shackles of iron, to carry out the sentence written against them—this is the glory of all his faithful people. Praise the LORD" (Psalm 149:1-9).

"... But you know him, for he lives with you and will be in you. I will not leave you as orphans; I will come to you. Before long, the world will not see me anymore, but you will see me. Because I live, you also will live. On that day you will realize that I am in my Father, and you are in me, and I am in you" (John 14:17-20).

"Then Peter said, 'Ananias, how is it that Satan has so filled your heart that you have lied to the Holy Spirit and have kept for yourself some of the money you received for the land? Didn't it belong to you before it was sold? And after it was sold, wasn't the money at your disposal? What made you think of doing such a thing? You have not lied just to human beings but to God'" (Acts 5:3, 4).

"And do not grieve the Holy Spirit of God, with whom you were sealed for the day of redemption" (Ephesians 4:30).

"But the fruit of the spirit is love, joy, peace, patience, kindness, goodness, faithfulness, gentleness and self-control ..." (Galatians 5:22, 23, ESV).

"You, my brothers and sisters, were called to be free. But do not use your freedom to indulge the flesh; rather, serve one another humbly in love. For the entire law is fulfilled in keeping this one command: 'Love your neighbor as yourself.' If you bite and devour each other, watch out or you will be destroyed by each other. So I say, walk by the Spirit, and you will not gratify the desires of the flesh. For the flesh desires what is contrary to the Spirit, and the Spirit what is contrary to the flesh. They are in conflict with each other, so that you are not to do whatever you want. But if the Spirit leads you, you are not under the law. The acts of the flesh are obvious: sexual immorality, impurity and debauchery; idolatry and witchcraft; hatred, discord, jealousy, fits of rage, selfish ambition, dissensions, factions and envy; drunkenness, orgies, and the like. I warn you, as I did before, that those who live like this will not inherit the kingdom of God. But the fruit of the Spirit is love, joy, peace, forbearance, kindness, goodness, faithfulness, gentleness and self-control. Against such things there is no law. Those who belong to Christ Jesus have crucified the flesh with its passions and desires. Since we live by the Spirit, let us keep in step with the Spirit. Let us not become conceited, provoking and envying each other" (Galatians 5:13-26).

"By their fruit you will recognize them. Do people pick grapes from thornbushes, or figs from thistles?" (Matthew 7:16).

"When the Advocate comes, whom I will send to you from the Father—the Spirit of truth who goes out from the Father—he will testify about me" (John 15:26).

"For the Word of God is alive and active. Sharper than any

double-edged sword, it penetrates even to dividing soul and spirit, joints and marrow; it judges the thoughts and attitudes of the heart" (Hebrews 4:12).

"… be filled with the Spirit, speaking to one another with psalms, hymns, and songs from the Spirit. Sing and make music from your heart to the Lord, always giving thanks to God the Father for everything, in the name of our Lord Jesus Christ" (Ephesians 5:18-20).

"The thief comes only to steal and kill and destroy; I have come that they may have life, and have it to the full" (John 10:10).

"Ascribe to the LORD the glory due His name; bring an offering and come before Him. Worship the LORD in the splendor of His holiness" (1 Chronicles 16:29).

"May the God who gives endurance and encouragement give you the same attitude of mind toward each other that Christ Jesus had, so that with one mind and one voice you may glorify the God and Father of our Lord Jesus Christ" (Romans 15:5, 6).

"But the LORD said to Samuel, 'Do not consider his appearance or his height, for I have rejected him. The LORD does not look at the things people look at. People look at the outward appearance, but the LORD looks at the heart'" (1 Samuel 16:7).

ABOUT THE AUTHOR

Alanderson Carvalho was born in Rio de Janeiro, Brazil, in 1979. He moved to the United States in the 90s when his father received an invitation to help plant a church in northern New Jersey. As he grew up, he was exposed to many different cultures and worship styles from living in a multicultural part of the U.S.

After accepting his vocational calling and identity from the Heavenly Father, he began an incredible journey with his beloved wife, Wanessa Bathke Carvalho. For the past ten years, they have been serving in several different ministries in the U.S. with one goal in mind—to help people BECOME WORSHIP. By becoming worship, he believes people will experience the Kingdom of God in a powerful way.

Alanderson current serves as the Worship Pastor and New Life Ministry Academy Overseer At New Life Church in Corpus Christi, Texas.

To contact Alan or to schedule a speaking engagement, go to:
Wpr.alanderson@gmail.com